CORPORATE STORM

A WHISTLEBLOWER'S FIGHT FOR JUSTICE
THROUGH ENTRENCHED CORRUPTION

Jennifer McGuire

First published by Ultimate World Publishing 2022
Copyright © 2022 Jennifer McGuire

ISBN

Paperback: 978-1-922714-96-1
Ebook: 978-1-922714-97-8

Jennifer McGuire has asserted her rights under the Copyright, Designs and Patents Act 1988 to be identified as the author of this work. The information in this book is based on the author's experiences and opinions. The publisher specifically disclaims responsibility for any adverse consequences which may result from use of the information contained herein. Permission to use information has been sought by the author. Any breaches will be rectified in further editions of the book.

All rights reserved. No part of this publication may be reproduced, stored in or introduced into a retrieval system, or transmitted in any form, or by any means (electronic, mechanical, photocopying, recording or otherwise) without the prior written permission of the author. Any person who does any unauthorised act in relation to this publication may be liable to criminal prosecution and civil claims for damages. Enquiries should be made through the publisher.

Cover design: Ultimate World Publishing
Layout and typesetting: Ultimate World Publishing
Editor: Isabelle Russell
Cover photo copyright license: Andrey_Kuzmin-Shutterstock.com

Ultimate World Publishing
Diamond Creek,
Victoria Australia 3089
www.writeabook.com.au

Dedication

Being a whistleblower is a very socially isolating experience. I have lost family and friends during this experience as they listened to rumours, and because of the confidentiality clauses of an investigation, I have been unable to discuss matters with them to straighten it out. Some of them just think I am an opinionated troublemaker who is here for a fight.

However, my closest family and friends have offered unwavering support and when they have heard rumours about me, they too have not had the knowledge or ability to set people straight but have always had my back and responded with words such as, 'If you knew Jen as well as I do you would know that she was standing up for someone else and what was right.'

Thanks to all those close family and friends who have had my back, especially my husband, Joe, and children, Annaliese, Eliza, Frazer and Harrison. I am writing this book so my grandchildren will get the true story and, seeing as this corruption involves a Government Owned Corporation, it is of public interest.

'I love the person I've become because I fought to become her.'
Kaci Diane

Contents

Dedication	iii
Foreword	1
Chapter 1: Storm Preparation	5
Chapter 2: A Storm is Brewing	29
Chapter 3: Thunder Roars	41
Chapter 4: Lightning Strikes	55
Chapter 5: Cyclonic Winds Blow	65
Chapter 6: The Eye of the Storm	79
Chapter 7: Batten Down the Hatches	91
Chapter 8: The Storm Front Builds	139
Chapter 9: Storm Clean-Up	147
Chapter 10: Skies Are Clearing	155
Epilogue	159
Resources	169
Referrals	173
Guest Speaker Bio	175
About the Author	176

Foreword

'Before us lies two paths – honesty and dishonesty. The short-sighted embark on the dishonest path; the wise on the honest. For the wise know the truth; in helping others we help ourselves; and in hurting others we hurt ourselves. Character overshadows money, and trust rises above fame. Honesty is still the best policy.'
Napoleon Hill

There will be many people who, when they read this book, will be gobsmacked by the myriad layers of inappropriate dealings, illegal behaviour and cronyism within a Government Owned Corporation, and they will be thankful that I have been brave enough to expose it to the general public and specifically to taxpayers. They, too, demand a change for the better. I thank you for your ongoing support.

On the other hand, there will be people who are ashamed of their actions and determined to continue to undermine my character, fabricate and spread malicious rumours behind my back and label me a 'squealer', 'whinger 'or 'snitch'. The people who truly know me know that I stood up for my personal values and the protection of others.

The final group will be those who recognise themselves in this book and head to the media to defend their actions or declare I am a liar. The only response I have for them is that I was in a low-level position at the Corporation, and I never benefited personally (financially or otherwise) from any interactions within my workplace. So, I had nothing to lose by exposing these cronies. Can these Executives say the same?

> *'There comes a time when one must take a position that is neither safe, nor popular, but he must take it because conscience tells him it is right.'*
> **Martin Luther King Jnr**

From a personal perspective, I wish to share what I discovered during this fight for justice because so many people before me took the hush money and walked away from the Corporation. The mental health practitioners that I have consulted during this fight have advised me that I am the only person they have supported that has stood up for what is right and not fled in fear. They went on to say that these people who took the hush money and were forced to sign a deed of confidentiality and waive their future rights would arrive in their practice with deteriorated mental health because, once they realised the reality of covering up the corruption and being unable to act from being gagged, they could no longer sleep at night and needed professional help. Consequently, they did what they thought they had to do at the time because they could see no other option.

I am writing this book to expose the alternate path that good people can take to end the ongoing cover-up of this kind of Executive bullying and corruption. I am seeking to remove the unknown, so that more people become aware of what else is available to them. It is my personal story, written from my perspective, so I do not assume the motivations or emotions of others.

Foreword

All the events covered in chapters 1 to 8 were discussed at my interview with the Crime and Corruption Commission (CCC) where I handed my four diaries' worth of notes and supporting materials over as evidence. I have a four-page letter I subsequently received from the CCC investigation process advising that all my allegations were substantiated. I do not go into the details of these claims, nor do I provide the evidence – this is to maintain the confidentiality of these investigation processes. In addition, I have not quoted names, times, dates, locations or other identifiers in order to protect those who deserve protection, wish to move past this upheaval and remain anonymous.

I have written my story to fill in the gaps of the many newspaper stories released across this time. I have the supporting documentation as evidence for all of the serious matters I write about in this book.

So, for all of you who were forced out of the Corporation after taking the hush money, I am writing this book for you too. The Executives' treatment of employees at the Corporation has been undoubtedly corrupt and caused great harm to those employees and their families. I hope this book helps you to heal, and that you know you were a precursor to creating the perfect storm for me to strike.

> 'She was powerful not because she wasn't scared but because she went on so strongly, despite her fear.'
> **Atticus**

CHAPTER 1

Storm Preparation

'Strong women aren't simply born. They are made by the storms they walk through.'
Anonymous

In my first week of work, I had a female team member arrive in my office in tears. At first, she was unable to talk because she was so visibly upset. I sat quietly with her around my conference table with my office door closed, handing her tissues, a glass of water and waiting for her to gain some composure and for her tears to start to dry up. Her chest was still heaving with unsettled breath, and she blurted out that she had just been groped on the breast by a male team member. She then unravelled again, and between the anger, the hurt and the tears I started to understand that she was newly single, aged in her mid-thirties and that the oldest male team member was pimping her out over the warehouse counter and she felt she had been taken advantage of.

At the time, I was equally as shocked by breast-groping in the workplace, but also perplexed by her accusation of being pimped out. At that stage, I had no idea of what she meant by it.

I had never encountered any behaviour like this in a large, industrial workplace before. I had worked with blokes all throughout the 25 years of my working life and the percentage of males to females in the organisations in which I worked was typically 90 per cent to 10 per cent at the most. I was always the only female in a leadership role, so I usually regarded the men in my crew as uncles or nephews and always formed a good working relationship with them. However, over the years I have seen women get burnt out very quickly when they decided to 'screw the crew' or flirt with their male teammates because, very quickly, the blokes would take advantage of their weakness and the woman would leave the workplace. The women who tended to cope the best in the male-dominated environment were those that worked in with the blokes, did not play the victim, did not use their sexuality to appeal and, most of all, they did their job well. What they lacked in brawn, they made up for in communication and the smarts to be able to bind the team together. I had only been in charge of the warehouse four days, so I had no idea of the team dynamic, but it did not matter anyway because the moment she told me I had a duty of care to act.

Once she took a breath and had calmed enough to dry her eyes and make eye contact with me, I had the chance to talk to her sensibly. When I told her that she needed to report this incident because it was sexual harassment, she responded that she could not because the old bloke would make her life hell. She had seen him do that to plenty of people before her and he was protected by the Union. I told her that I did not have a choice as her leader because sexual harassment is illegal under the Workplace Health & Safety legislation. So, off we walked to human resources to open a massive can of worms and my fiery introduction to the harmful workplace I had just joined.

****

The first activity undertaken by a good leader when starting a new job is to read all the policy, standards, procedures and work Instructions of

Storm Preparation

a new workplace. As you very quickly get a lay of the land and how you are required to interact successfully within the business. Everything I opened in the Corporation's electronic document system or on their internal internet was either out of date or under review or there was nothing to cover the topic. For instance, an integrated safety management system did not exist. My new team did not even have the legislated risk management documents that had been legally required for a decade by the Workplace Health and Safety legislation. The Corporation had no management processes for fatality prevention hazards, such as confined space, work at heights, machinery guarding, traffic management and their electrical isolation process involved people using their messy handwriting on an isolation permit document which led to the confusion in identification of what equipment to isolate and maintenance people and contractors working on live plant, such as conveyors.

Seeing as there was no safety management system, there were no inspections to be undertaken in the workplace to ensure the equipment and the environment was safe. Vehicle pre-start checklists were optional before operating mobile equipment, there were no crane lift plans and people relied on the most experienced worker that had been at the Corporation the longest to explain how things were done. Because of the lack of management system to describe the best way, or the only way, the employees used to argue among themselves on how to approach a job. Needless to say, the Corporation's injury statistics were the worst I have ever encountered and double other similar industry statistics.

****

Within those first two weeks of starting my new job, I also discovered that as the team leader I had to complete my team's individual timesheets. I had never seen anything like this anywhere else I had ever worked. Everywhere else I had worked, employees were told, 'This is a legal timesheet document for you to complete accurately, submit to your supervisor to review and approve on time to enable you to get paid.' This was going to be an onerous task each week for me to ensure that I accurately captured all 13 team members time spent in the workplace, and then there would be the payroll discrepancies that they would enquire about. So, they had no responsibility for their workplace attendance records.

The first action I undertook was to read the Enterprise Bargaining Agreement and then gain a report of each person's electronic gate access to the Corporation so that I could understand the hours they were supposed to be working compared to what they were actually working. What a vast number of discrepancies I uncovered. People were starting and finishing work earlier than required. Some were leaving work unauthorised for hours during the middle of a shift. The pimp of an old team member had adopted a completely different rostered day off to the rest of the team, simply because that is what he had always done. While the worst case of time rip off was the 'job and knock' approach to an employee's time at the Corporation. These were the people that thought they had done enough for the day, so they left the workplace without notification or approval. Another hornet's nest was unveiled.

****

The first three months of my new job were a difficult adjustment period. I had to rewind the way I worked 20 years ago. I began to wonder what the Corporation had been doing for the past decades, and whether their Executive had fallen asleep on the job and not kept up with the legal requirements and cost-effectiveness required of a modern workplace. As I started to get my feet under the desk, I soon realised things were a lot worse than what I had already encountered.

The asset management system sat as paperwork in a folder on the general manager's bookshelf. When I went to create preventative maintenance

Storm Preparation

cycles for the routine inspection and service of the equipment and facilities, I was responsible for – this had never been done. It was a run-to-failure business without any activities planned and actioned according to schedule. It represented yet another dawning of how far behind the Corporation was from comparative industry and how the Corporation was not focused on profitability, productivity or waste minimisation.

I started to notice on my regular walk-through inspections that on a Monday morning the warehouse consumable products would be missing from the shelves. It became apparent that during afterhours shifts items such as coffee, tea, milk, sugar, stationery, batteries, tape, sunscreen, paper towel and bottled water would be significantly depleted. This minority of employees were taking household items and perhaps didn't have a second thought, because we all worked for a large corporation. Perhaps they thought it wouldn't be noticed? On top of this, during the week, I witnessed employees leaving the warehouse with not just one pair of safety glasses for their day, but handfuls of them. It seemed that every day, some employees would go through a full set of personal protective equipment after each morning tea, lunch or afternoon tea break. These employees were contributing to a disposable workplace full of waste and ultimately wasting money.

One morning upon arriving to work, I saw one of these potential shoplifters leaving the workplace main pedestrian turnstile with a 1kg tin of coffee under each arm, so I stopped him to ask where he was going with them. He was very quick to tell me where to get off as he headed for the carpark. This minority of employees were taking items beyond their own personal use. So, I did the only thing I could to try to alleviate the waste, and I created reports for management to show the excessive consumable consumption. The reports revealed that an employee a week consumed a 1kg caterer's tin of coffee.

I did not realise how uneconomical the Corporation was until the 'Webber Gate' scandal came to light. It was covered in newspapers:

THE OBSERVER

Monday, April 3, 2017

By Chris Lees

Port ripped off through their own scheme

GLADSTONE Ports Corporation has been ripped off through its Health and Wellbeing Reimbursement Scheme.

Employee #1 appeared in Gladstone Magistrates Court yesterday, charged with false entry in record

The scheme is a program to cover costs of health and wellbeing products and activities.

Gladstone Port. Gladstone Observer

Outside of court police prosecutor Gavin Reece said Employee #1 bought a barbecue from a store for himself and told GPC the money had been spent on fishing rods.

Mr Reece said GPC reimbursed him for what they thought were fishing rods.

Employee #1, 58, pleaded guilty, was fined $400 and had paid back the cost of the barbecue. In a statement Ports said it had been made aware of potential irregularities in claims made by some employees under the Health and Wellbeing Reimbursement Scheme.

"As required under the provisions of the Crime and Corruption Act (2001), the Corporation reports any allegations of misconduct to the Crime and Corruption Commission (CCC) and if appropriate, the Queensland Police Service (QPS)," the statement read.

GPC chief executive officer Peter O'Sullivan said they treated claims of fraudulent behaviour or misconduct with concern.

"GPC has conducted a full internal investigation into this matter and as a result raised the issue with the QPS," he said.

The statement said as the matter is before the courts, they could not comment on any particular aspect of the investigations.

Police said investigations were ongoing into the matter. More people are expected to face the court in coming days on similar charges.

CORPORATE STORM

THE OBSERVER

Monday, April 10, 2017

By Sarah Barnham

BREAKING: GPC worker guilty on dodgy bbq claims

ANOTHER Gladstone Ports Corporation worker faced court today on Health and Wellbeing Scheme rorts charges.

Employee #2 tried to claim $300 for a barbecue using falsified records.

Employee #2 pleaded guilty to the Gladstone Magistrates Court on one charge of imposition after submitting falsified records in a reimbursement claim to the GPC, under the corporation's Health and Wellbeing Scheme.

The scheme allows GPC staff to be reimbursed for up to $299 in goods that contribute to their well-being, like fishing rods and reels.

There is a set list of items that can, and cannot be reimbursed which was given to all workers. The Observer has been unable to obtain a copy of this list.

Employee #2, 48, was just a small fish in a big pond of about 82 other GPC workers, who used dodgy documents to try to claim back money for products they bought, but were not entitled to claim under the scheme.

Storm Preparation

Three GPC workers, Employee #3, Employee #4 and Employee #1, faced court last week on the same charges. All three workers received fines of $400.

The court heard Employee #2 tried to claim the four-burner barbecue using receipts that showed purchase of fishing rods and reels from the Gladstone Camping Centre.

Defence lawyer Axel Beard said the list of items workers could claim was "arbitrary" and he had heard that while workers could be reimbursed for a new motorbike tyre, they couldn't for a motorbike helmet.

He said while Employee #2 was aware he fraudulently filled out reimbursement forms and handed them in, he had yet to be reimbursed by the GPC before the corporation began to investigate workers' claims.

"He received no benefit from the act," Mr Beard said.

"It seems to be a cultural issue between the corporation and workers, my client received a written warning for his actions, but still keeps his job."

Acting Gladstone Magistrate Neil Lavaring fined Employee #2 $300 with no conviction recorded.

THE OBSERVER

Thursday, May 25, 2017

Another GPC worker busted over false claims

A 62-year-old Gladstone man with absolutely no criminal history found himself before court for the first time on Tuesday.

Employee #5 was just one of about 80 Gladstone Ports Corporation workers who used falsified documents to complete a reimbursement application.

He pleaded guilty in the Gladstone Magistrates Court to one charge of false entry in record.

Through the GPC's Health and Wellbeing Reimbursement Scheme, workers are entitled to purchase items and then be reimbursed under a program to cover costs of health and well-being products and activities.

However, there is a list of items that can and cannot be reimbursed, which according to the GPC, was made clear to workers.

Despite this a number of GPC staff purchased items not covered under the scheme and provided false receipts on their reimbursement forms which stated otherwise.

But GPC caught wind of these false claims, and after a search warrant was executed at a Gladstone store with the real receipts uncovered, a long list of names were set to face court.

The court heard Employee #5 purchased a $99.95 Annexe mat, but used a false receipt stating he had purchased a bush fishing rod for the same amount.

He agreed to pay back the full amount he was reimbursed for by GPC.

Defence lawyer Axel Beard said his client was one of many workers confused by what they could and could not claim under the scheme.

He said his client had been placed on a good behaviour bond by the company.

Gladstone magistrate Melanie Ho said she was aware many of his colleagues were in the same boat and would therefore convict him with the same punishment.

Employee #5 left the courtroom with a $400 fine.

THE OBSERVER

Wednesday, July 12, 2017

By Sarah Barnham

Gladstone ports workers face court over false claims

ONE FORMER and two present Gladstone Ports Corporation workers faced Gladstone Magistrates Court after using false receipts to claim money they weren't entitled to.

It was just a few of many similar cases that have already been heard or are yet to be heard by the courts after an investigation conducted by the GPC revealed workers were taking advantage of the company's Health and Wellbeing Scheme, which allows workers to purchase goods and be reimbursed for them.

However, the scheme only allows workers to purchase specific items that directly contribute to the worker's health and well-being, for example a kayak.

But workers were buying items from a Gladstone store that did not fall under the scheme, however in their reimbursement applications they used falsified receipts to make it look as if they did.

A search warrant of the store executed by police located the falsified documents.

Storm Preparation

A number of GPC workers have already faced the court, with at least 80 charged on the same offence of false entry in record.

This week, a 62-year-old worker with no criminal history pleaded guilty to the charge of false entry in record, but unlike his colleagues he'd tried to crack the system twice.

Employee #6 made two purchases at the Gladstone store, one in 2014 and again in 2015.

Both times he used false receipts to be reimbursed for the items, worth more than $600.

The court heard he had been employed at the company for 12 years, had two adult children and was a married man of 43 years.

Like his colleagues, Employee #6 was issued a warning from the company and was made to pay back what he was falsely reimbursed for.

Gladstone magistrate Melanie Ho ordered him to pay an $800 fine but did not record a conviction.

Co-offenders Employee #7, 21, and Employee #8 pleaded guilty to the same charge.

The court heard the pair were in a relationship and purchased items from the store worth up to $900 on the same day.

Defence lawyer Rio Ramos said both of them were under the impression "everyone was doing it".

Ms Ramos said Employee #7 received a warning from the company, however Employee #8 now worked for himself.

Despite this, both had paid back the amount they had been reimbursed for.

The pair were both fined $400, with no convictions recorded.

CORPORATE STORM

THE OBSERVER

Saturday, May 5, 2018

By Andrew Thorpe

More GPC workers guilty of rorting health scheme

FOUR more Gladstone Ports Corporation employees have pleaded guilty to rorting the company's Health and Wellbeing Reimbursement Scheme.

The men did not appear in person at Gladstone Magistrates Court on Tuesday, instead pleading guilty in writing to charges of placing a false entry in record.

It was revealed last year that about 80 employees had been caught taking advantage of the company through the scheme.

It was intended to encourage staff to purchase goods for outdoor recreation that would help their health and fitness.

Under the scheme, GPC would reimburse workers up to $299 for a range of equipment, which included fishing rods.

But for several years, employees were purchasing items not covered by the scheme and providing false receipts on reimbursement forms.

When GPC caught wind of the scheme, a search warrant was executed at a store and the real receipts were uncovered.

Storm Preparation

Previous claims included a four-burner barbecue and an annexe floor mat being passed off as fishing rods.

Of the four men who pleaded guilty on Tuesday, one had rorted the scheme three times, another twice, and the remaining two once each.

One of the men, who had bought an esky and claimed it as fishing equipment, told the court he regretted the decision and had since paid back the money. He was fined $400.

The same punishment was handed out to a man who had claimed he had bought a kayak under the scheme.

The man who rorted the scheme twice said he had also paid the money back to GPC but the experience had still tarnished his employment record and caused stress to his family.

He was fined $800 for falsely claiming $600 for a fishing rod/kayak combo package.

The man who rorted the scheme three times - also including a false claim for a fishing rod/kayak combo package - was fined $1200.

No convictions were recorded in any of the cases.

A fifth man was scheduled to appear on Tuesday on the same charge.

CORPORATE STORM

THE OBSERVER

Saturday, November 17, 2018

Business owner in GPC compensation rort faces $10,000 fine

Gladstone Camping Centre owner Brett Bowman leaves court with consultant solicitor Barry Ross. Mike Richards GLA161118CURT
17th Nov 2018 8:00 AM
Subscriber only

THE owner of a Gladstone business that issued false receipts to Gladstone Ports Corporation workers in a bid to rort the corporation's health scheme is facing a $10,000 fine.

Storm Preparation

Gladstone Camping Centre owner Brett Wesley Bowman pleaded guilty in Gladstone Magistrates Court to one charge of the intent to defraud by producing a number of receipts, knowing they were false, namely of products sold.

The court heard the offending involved about 78 GPC workers over four years between October, 2012, and September, 2016.

In 2017 investigations revealed GPC workers using the corporation's Health and Wellbeing Reimbursement Scheme incorrectly.

The scheme is a program to cover costs of health and wellbeing products and activities.

Under the scheme, GPC reimbursed workers up to $299 for equipment purchased, including fishing rods.

The purchase receipts and a compensation claim form would be filed with GPC and the employee would be reimbursed for the purchase.

But the scheme only allowed workers to be reimbursed for certain items.

Workers were being issued two receipts by Gladstone Camping Centre - the real document and a false.

An example used in court was one employee who bought a barbecue but was issued a false receipt that stated he purchased fishing rods.

Fishing rods were allowed under the scheme but the barbecue was not.

The worker was reimbursed by GPC compensation to which he was not entitled.

The court heard 83 false receipts produced by Gladstone Camping Centre were issued to workers to receive compensation payouts.

Police prosecutor Joel Sleep said Bowman had no criminal history and was a respectable man in the community.

Mr Sleep said the 55-year-old was facing charges that carried a maximum 10 years imprisonment.

Instead of jail time, Mr Sleep said it would be more appropriate to fine Bowman a sum of $10,000.

VAJ Byrne and Co Lawyers consultant solicitor Barry Ross asked the Magistrate not to fine his client nor record a conviction.

Mr Ross told Magistrate Dennis Kinsella he could produce supporting documents to show there were issues in the compiling of evidence against his client.

He also said without his client's assistance, police would have had a difficult time building a case against Bowman.

Mr Ross said GPC was a substantial corporation with about 700 employees. He compared it to Bowman's business of five employees, including himself and his wife.

Mr Ross told the court the GPC's scheme had fallen into "non-management" and employees did not know they were doing the wrong thing.

He said his client was unaware the receipts were being used in a filing process. Mr Ross told the court following the offending, the 78 workers involved in the rort were at threat of unemployment.

Mr Ross did not present any documents to the court, however, told Mr Kinsella he could access them if needed.

Mr Ross said before the police investigation began, a number of GPC staff members visited Bowman's store to "demand" an explanation into the offending.

Mr Kinsella told Mr Ross if he planned to substantiate and elaborate on the claims he would need to adjourn the matter to allow it more time.

Mr Kinsella said he did not want to rush Mr Ross and adjourned the guilty plea sentence part heard. The matter will be continued before the court on November 30.

THE OBSERVER

Monday, December 3, 2018

Lawyer blames GPC 'mismanagement' in compensation rort

DESPITE a lawyer's best efforts to convince a magistrate his client was mostly innocent in a four-year compensation rort, a Gladstone business owner has been fined $5000.

Gladstone Camping Centre owner Brett Wesley Bowman previously pleaded guilty in Gladstone Magistrates Court to one charge of the intent to defraud by producing a number of receipts, knowing they were false, namely of products sold.

The sentence was adjourned part-heard and brought back before the court on Friday.

The court heard Bowman's offending involved several Gladstone Ports Corporation workers over four years between October, 2012 and September, 2016. In 2017 investigations revealed GPC workers using the corporation's Health and Wellbeing Reimbursement Scheme incorrectly, using false receipts issued by Bowman's business.

The scheme is a program to cover costs of health and wellbeing products and activities.

Under the scheme, GPC reimbursed workers up to $299 for equipment purchased, including fishing rods.

The purchase receipts and a compensation claim form would be filed with GPC and the employee would be reimbursed for the purchase.

But the scheme only allowed workers to be reimbursed for certain items.

Workers were being issued two receipts by Bowman, 56 and his employees at Gladstone Camping Centre - the real document and a false.

Employees were using the false receipt to claim compensation they were not entitled to. The court heard Bowman's business issued 83 false receipts.

Consultant solicitor Barry Ross said although the GPC had "written themselves as victims", Bowman and the GPC employees were the real victims.

Mr Ross said the GPC mismanaged the scheme to the point employees were unaware that what they were doing was wrong.

He said in several witness statements employees said they "felt sick" about using the fake receipts and "had no idea they were doing the wrong thing".

But this was contradicted by other witness statements which revealed it was common knowledge among employees that the Gladstone Camping Store was the business to go to for false receipts.

Magistrate Dennis Kinsella said it was also a "double-edged sword".

Mr Kinsella said the "mismanagement" of the scheme was taken advantage of by Bowman and the GPC workers.

Mr Ross argued that his client did not know the forms were being used in a claiming process.

He also said there were deficiencies in the evidence against his client and said GPC workers were "pressured" by the company to give evidence.

Storm Preparation

Mr Kinsella said it was clear Bowman was aware of the fraud, given he issued GPC worker two receipts, including a false one.

The court heard Bowman could have been fined $10,000 for the offending but Mr Ross asked for no penalty.

He said if there must be a fine, that it be no more than the $300-$400 that the GPC workers were issued for the offending.

But Mr Kinsella said Bowman's offending was of a larger scale and over a long period of time.

He said Bowman was a "cog" in the greater scheme.

Mr Kinsella imposed a $5000 fine, but did not record a conviction.

The 'Webber Gate' incident initially involved 82 employees taking advantage of the Corporation by falsely claiming purchases under the Corporation's health and wellbeing scheme. This employee benefit was intended to encourage staff to purchase goods for outdoor recreation that would help their health and fitness. Under the scheme, the Corporation would reimburse workers up to $299 for a range of health and fitness equipment, including fishing rods.

However, for several years thereafter, employees were purchasing items not covered by the scheme and providing false receipts on reimbursement forms.

When the Corporation became aware of potential irregularities in claims, the Executive commenced an internal investigation. I had no knowledge of anything at the time and was not the whistleblower for this matter. However, as a leader of an employee that had rorted the scheme, I was not advised of any information officially by the Executive. The whole investigation was kept at the highest level. The only information I received was from the alleged fraudster worried about what this might mean to their future employment.

The accused were represented by their union and provided statements to read out in which they did not accept any responsibility, nor make any kind of confession or apology. Many of the fraudsters were from the same union, and those alleged told me that they were encouraged by their union representative to undertake this deception because the representative would provide their union members with falsified receipts. They explained that it the union representative said it was so easy that they had done it year upon year, and instead of getting a yoga mat, stretch bands or weights under the scheme, they got what they wanted, like a barbeque.

By the end of the internal investigation, I was half expecting to see people terminated; because this would send a very strong message to the people

Storm Preparation

rorting the process; including most of the unions who thought their members and reps were untouchable. Instead, the fraudsters received a written warning and, as required under the provisions of the Crime and Corruption Act (2001), the Corporation reported the allegations of misconduct to the CCC and where appropriate, to the Police Service. So, a search warrant was executed at a store and the real receipts were uncovered. The employees then appeared in the Magistrates Court, charged with false entry in record.

Many of the fraudulent employees pleaded guilty to multiple counts of rorting the scheme; some three and four times. They were usually fined $400 per false claim and ordered to pay each $299 false claim back to the Corporation. No convictions were recorded in any of the cases.

The interesting part to this deeply entrenched fraud is that the Corporation CEO was previously the Labor Party candidate in 2009 State Election. After his failed bid for the seat, he commenced working in the Government Owned Corporation. After these 82 initial rorters were uncovered, further investigation was requested by the other unions, as these 82 fraudsters all purchased their equipment from a single store, so imagine how many other businesses were involved in this rort and how many other Corporation employees (and their partner's or family's businesses made money as a result) were involved in this systemic rip off from taxpayers' money. Requests by the other unions to broaden the scope of the investigation were always denied by the Executive.

I only claimed my health and wellbeing benefit once, and I still enjoy the pleasure of fishing with my rod and reel to this day. I have never worked for an organisation that gives you $299 a year to spend on yourself. The most I have ever received was a smoked leg of ham for Christmas and my family were delighted with this gift.

> *'Smooth seas never made a skilled sailor.'*
> **Franklin D Roosevelt**

CHAPTER 2

A Storm is Brewing

*'Not all storms come to disrupt your life,
some come to clear your path.'*
Anonymous

After working at the Corporation for a couple of months, it was time to start implementing the improvements I had identified during my rough start. Among the items that first needed to be implemented were within the team development area, because of the impact of the 'pimping' over the warehouse counter. Which at this point in time I still had no idea what she meant by the term 'pimping her out'? And because some employees had turned over due to this incident, it was time to reset and gain alignment. I started the process to engage a team-building facilitator to help me at an offsite venue, along with catering, and here is where I came up against a heap of run-around for something so simple.

I started looking around the Corporation's electronic document system or on their intranet and I could only locate an incredibly old Tendering Manual created by an external consultant engaged to write the desktop 'how-to guide' way back in 2004. It was never implemented, but even if it had been, the processes did not currently exist in the business for me to follow. In fact, this Tendering Manual was written in such high-level, general, theoretical terms that it created more confusion and arguments in the business than provide direction.

I read through the Tendering Manual and could not find anything relevant to help me in procuring services, venue or catering to host the team development workshops. As such, I contacted the procurement team to get the run around between each procurement officer; because this training was for the warehouse team, so should it go via the human resources' training team. 'Oh no, they don't have a contract for team development consultants,' I was told. 'You need to get a quote for the services and send it to the procurement officer in an email, and then we can give you a purchase order,' they continued. 'But what if I do not know how long this team development is going to take?' 'Well,' they said, 'you will have to get another quote and send it to us on email and then we will give you another purchase order.' 'Okay. So, what do I do about venue hire?' I asked. 'You will have to get your general manager's executive assistant to organise a venue because procurement officers do not do that.' 'Then, what about the catering?' I pressed. 'Do you have a catering contract I can use to organise food for the workshops?' Again, I was told, 'No, procurement officers do not do that. You organise the catering, get the invoice, and then accounts will pay it for you.'

Seeing how the organisation of team development training had created such ambiguity and complexity around something so simple, I thought I would select something at the other end of the spectrum that was way more critical to see what commercial arrangement was in place – fuel. The Corporation was the fourth largest fuel consumer in the State, and without fuel, the Corporation's mobile assets would stop and operations would cease. What commercial arrangement does the procurement team have in place for the fuel inventory that I am responsible for? Nothing!

A Storm is Brewing

No commercial agreement at all. Instead, the fuel supplier sent in a monthly invoice to be paid.

This was another dawning of how far behind the Corporation was from comparative industry and how the Corporation was not focused on profitability, productivity or waste minimisation.

****

Over the next couple of weeks, I started to gather information about the lack of commercial arrangements and began to understand how much flexibility employees had in their purchase of materials and equipment. Each department general manager operated their business differently to each other without co-ordinating any effort between them. This meant that one department using a crane would engage crane business A on a daily rate while another department would engage crane business B on an hourly rate and never co-ordinate between them to become more cost effective to benefit the business. I started to hear historic stories of Corporation project supervisors buying cranes that they would hire back via a contractor and share the profit. I heard stories of the Corporation's supervisors getting their relatives' earthworks business to do the entire Corporation's excavation jobs across many years without ever testing the market. Anytime I spoke to anyone about why they used a certain contractor for services, or why they purchased materials from a certain vendor, it was because they knew the Corporation's business.

The reverse was once again the lack of a risk management approach to the Corporation's procurement. Some of these contractors and vendors provided production critical services and materials, so what commercial arrangements were in place to ensure that the critical items were delivered to the quality, time at the agreed price? In the instance of cranes – nothing. If the Corporation needed a certain size crane, with a certain length of boom reach for an operational breakdown, then it was the goodwill of the crane company to make it to the site in a timely manner and then they would send in their invoice afterwards.

The inventory replenishment in the warehouse was also purchase order to purchase order. Every time an inventory item needed to be restocked, a quotation was sought from the favoured vendor and a purchase order sent for the vendor to provide the materials.

I soon discovered that the Corporation was doing business with themselves and there was a mountain of repetitive administration effort instead of a cost-effective approach. To support this observation, I started to accumulate the transactional history from the accounting department. From this invoice payment history, I could very quickly see that most of the business was in transactional day-to-day purchases and hardly any contracts existed. Typically, invoices arrived in the accounts department just in time for payment, after the service or material had been delivered by the vendor.

During this fact-finding mission, the most sinister aspect I discovered was this very old commercial agreement template the Corporation called a 'standing offer'. This standing offer format was used when the Corporation did not award a purchase order. Both these forms of contract terms and conditions were very dated and no longer legally compliant or able to protect the Corporation in any way if challenged. The standing offer was fundamentally a noticeably brief list of agreed standard terms; the most important one to the Corporation employee wanting the services was the timing or term and the list of the schedule of rates. The rest were just payment terms and general clauses dealing with matters such as dispute resolution, termination and liability that were all out of date. It was essentially a stand-by agreement that usually a government department, such as child safety uses by setting up a panel of providers for emergency engagements, such as crisis accommodation provision. This means that across a location, several motels may have

A Storm is Brewing

a standing offer in place for several years with agreed rates to be used when a child is at risk and needs to be removed and accommodated short term for their safety and until an ongoing arrangement can be identified and secured.

The Corporation was operating largely on purchase orders for materials and standing offers for services. In the project engineering department, the standing offers were provided to the same four mechanical contractors, the same four civil contractors, the same four electrical contractors to be used year in year out. If you asked anyone in the project engineering departments why they used these same contractors all the time, they would respond that they knew the Corporation's business.

The procurement function was an administration effort and did not add any value to the business. There was loads of room for improvement.

****

The way in which I prefer to work is to put my money where my mouth is and make a proposal. I am not a person that sits back throws rocks and complains. I always strive to be part of a solution. In keeping with my comfortable work style, I created a scope of work document, titled Procure to Pay to identify the limitations of a non-existent procurement process that outlined to all employees what they needed to do to buy goods or services at the Corporation. I escalated this scope of work to the Executive and was called to a meeting. The general manager I reported to wanted me to implement a process and put contracts in place that would help his (or our own) department. Other general managers had been at the Corporation for most of their senior career, so they were used to micromanaging and determining what vendors their employees would continually engage. They did not want anything to change, so they asked how they would be kept informed of purchases, and if they could still order a taxi and pay when they were at the Brisbane office, why couldn't they continue to organise their own purchases however they liked? This disjointed approach would prove difficult because the whole Corporation needed a single integrated way to do business, a common process to follow that would open the Corporation to the outside market. The commercial general manager knew that he was responsible for this management system across the entire business, and he wanted me to be seconded to work for him to design, implement and train people in it.

After many months of meetings to discuss this initiative, I was eventually asked to reprioritise from my normal position to work on the procure to pay management system (PTP) development. I quickly described to the Executive how this was not a part-time job and that little could be achieved until it was resourced appropriately. I did not believe they understood the enormity of the task at hand and that they welcomed the change. I felt I was being set up to fail so as nothing would alter and the current, comfortable arrangements would remain unchanged. As a result, I had to think on my feet to skin the cat differently and recommend an alternative solution of engaging an external, independent consultant to put together a current state document and recommend the changes required for the Executive to consider. If there was one thing I had learnt over the decades, it was that when an Executive cannot see the forest for the trees, they will listen to an external party ahead of an employee. I recommended the Corporation engage independent consulting services from Rsured* in the first instance to start to understand the current state of the business. I had engaged this business at other industrial sites in the past and therefore, I knew they would be able to provide the Executive a holistic approach to provide them a detailed current status and recommend future requirements. These future requirements could then be scoped and taken to the open marketplace once they were known and detailed.

---

* https://rsured.com/ your single integrated business management system

A Storm is Brewing

The Executive agreed to engage Rsured and requested that I organise the engagement and current state mapping process. However, the Executive did not provide any communications to the business about the current state mapping exercise that was about to be undertaken. It was all news to everyone and due to this lack of providing senior leadership support, context and purpose the first workshops were met with a lot of resistance from people. The rough start to implement change continued.

****

I scheduled these workshops to include people from all parts of the business. I intentionally invited people from all levels and all functions to be in the same sessions. A session could have a production manager, environmental specialist, corporate secretarial support, accountant, maintenance trade supervisor, marine pilot and engineer. I arranged for a member of the procurement team to attend every workshop so as they could understand the pain the business was feeling and the impact on the business from their lack of a consistent way of doing business.

After the first two workshops, I received two complaints from two different members of the Executive. The first complaint was, why are you not putting all my people in a room together because I am getting too many questions from my team members after these workshops. The second complaint was that the Rsured consultant was asking too many questions and people were becoming defensive about how they did things – I knew we were on the right path.

By the third workshop, word had got out across the business of what we were up to and what was taking place in the room. People had recognised that, for the first time, they were being sat in a room from different parts and levels of the business to talk about how they go about doing something. In this case it was how they go about requesting a material or a service and then pay for it. Those who did not arrive at the earlier workshop they were scheduled to attend asked to join other sessions. People sat in these sessions and identified all the problems they had in buying materials and services and then in paying for them. They shared their frustrations and sometimes other attendees had the solutions and shared how they went about successfully getting things done. The disparity, flexibility, optionality and chaos within in the business were clearly visible to everyone. The procurement staff would argue with the attendees on the right way of doing things, arguing among themselves even. By the end of the workshops, people were asking for a single way – the best way – to buy materials and services to end the confusion and make their lives easier.

To cut a long story short, we spent many months putting a new PTP management system together with Rsured consultants engaged fulltime and myself part-time, with an Executive sponsor to oversee our effort, and by consulting all areas of the business, and building the system with procurement and accounting people. We gave many presentations to the Executive to keep them informed of our progress and when it came time to implement and train the business, I was seconded to the commercial department fulltime. So, I went from operating the warehouse and site services team to include the supply team.

By the implementation phase, the Chief Executive Officer was so supportive of the PTP implementation that he wanted it done yesterday and even produced a video of him directing the Corporation in its mandatory use, highlighting the legal compliance and supporting its implementation. He also wanted me to train staff in the business because of my skills, experience and personal intimate knowledge of the system.

At the same time as running the PTP training, I was working with a whole new team of procurement people in supply and had to work with them to ensure they were handling the massive changes to how they went about their work. It was the largest amount of change I have ever had to manage without specialist resources being applied. However, this organic, hands-on approach resulted in the uncovering of many unethical, illegal, fraudulent and corrupt undertakings because people approached me confidentially after the training to highlight areas of non-compliance, such as:

- Those in supervisory positions sending multiple and regular works to their family members' businesses over many years duration.
- Independent contractors were able to create work orders in the computer system to continue to engage them and create future work for themselves.
- A member of the Executive who was fulfilling a fulltime, permanent general manager position for the Corporation was not only engaged through his independent contracting business but also his Executive assistant and other key team members were contracted into Corporation traditionally permanent roles. The general manager was earning a profit margin every hour he and his key team members worked.
- Eleven independent contractors had been engaged at the corporation to fulfil equivalent corporation fulltime, permanent jobs. They earnt almost twice the amount of their corporation peer. All of them had been engaged for over two years and one had been engaged for over seven years and another was paid more than the Australian Prime Minister to be a project control accountant; and
- Ten owner truck drivers hauled product every day for twice the amount a normal contracted truck driver would earn. These guys had been doing this for decades and when the individual owner driver decided to retire, he would hand the truck and the Corporation's business onto his successor. This contracted work never went to an open market to give other truck drivers or transport businesses the opportunity to win a contract fairly.

Corporate Storm

During the implementation and training of the new PTP management system, there were many smaller illegal and non-compliant activities unearthed. People were starting to understand why a separation of duties was necessary in a commercial transaction, what a conflict of interest was and what probity in procurement meant – ethical behaviour! During these early weeks of the new system, perhaps the worst interaction I experienced with an unethical procurement involved the human resources general manager.

She had requested a tender process to source Indigenous cultural awareness training to be provided in the Corporation. She was very driven to have this implementation in accordance with the Corporation's reconciliation action plan. The part that I tried to explain to her was her competitive approach to a very niche market was supporting one entity ahead of the others. In her tender, she had requested the five local indigenous tribal organisations to bid against each other to provide cultural awareness training. I struggled for her to accept my commercial advice that it was biased for the behemoth Corporation to request that Indigenous tribes compete against one another and then the Corporation would select one tribe ahead of the others and promote and develop them for their *own gain*. I challenged her on several occasions that this was like asking the Catholic Church to teach religious education in schools on behalf of the Jehovah's Witnesses, Seventh Day Adventists and Baptists – you get the picture. I was only met with resistance from her. I then discovered she was having coffee meetings with the CEO of one of the Aboriginal corporations requested to bid during this tender process and went as far as to direct me to award the tender to his Aboriginal corporation even though the supply team had not completed the bid evaluations and the Aboriginal corporation concerned had not submitted a complying bid.

During one of my meetings with her to try to teach her the PTP requirements and show her the legally compliant way, she threatened to give me the sack. At the time I was taken back and thought this was just another senior manager not liking the change. But little did I know at the time, she had put a target on my back.

> *'She stood in the storm, and when it did not blow her way, she adjusted her sails.'*
> **Elizabeth Edwards**

CHAPTER 3

Thunder Roars

*'Thunder is good, thunder is impressive;
but it is lightening that does all the work.'*
Mark Twain

The implementation of a business wide system without any additional resources was the most challenging time in my 25-plus-year career. It involved a lot of long hours and I had people around me asking if I was Superwoman. I was thriving as I realised changes through all my hard work and effort. Since I am a 'completer' personality type, I had a second wind in the marathon and knew that I would finish strongly and be pleased with a job well done.

I was being praised by my immediate general manager and thanked by the supply team of procurement officers that they finally knew what work was heading their way and they had a whole suite of documents and processes to use. The resistance among supply team members had been resolved and people were starting to relax into their new reality. I engaged an independent consultant to help me work with the team on some teambuilding exercises and I arranged one on one coaching for those team members who wanted to undertake some personal development training. Some team members leant into this offer because they understood the previous anarchy in which they worked was caused by the lack of a systemised approach to their jobs. The continual arguments had left the bullies to rule and there was no cooperation within the team. Now that they had a system to apply, some team members were keen to mend relationships and learn how to work together.

This new norm allowed me to spend more time in my original position in the warehouse team. Unfortunately, while I had been distracted across months on my massive workload, the union members had started to play again.

I returned to the warehouse only to find the new school leaving female trainee in tears. At first, she was too scared to talk to me about her treatment. But after some days had passed, she finally updated me on the bullying and intimidating behaviour she had been experiencing from the same union representative that had offered to pimp out the previous female team member. However, this was now a worse case, because the only other female team member that had previously feared this old bully bloke had now joined in with him and his inappropriate behaviour.

I interviewed the other team members to find out what had been happening while I had been distracted implementing the new system, and I found out that this old union rep and his newfound friend a union member that had defrauded the Corporation during Webber Gate, had ganged up on this young female trainee and had managed to make her work life hell. For instance, instead of helping her to learn to operate the warehouse electric stock picker, he would stand at the end of an aisle with his large arms crossed, just staring at her as she went about her task. If she were at a warehouse computer searching the catalogue for intricate, complex named maintenance parts, he would not ask if she needed help; he would instead stand behind her, looking over her shoulder. The female union member he now had under his control would booby-trap jobs that the trainee was expected to do, so as she would have to work harder or clean things up, or demand jobs that normally took two hours to be done in half the time. The two of them spread gossip about the trainee by complaining to everyone they met that she was the laziest trainee they had even encountered and that she was only employed because she was my daughter's best friend.

The fact of the matter was that this school leaving female went through the Corporation's recruitment process that involved an interview panel of three people, which included myself as the immediate team supervisor, another warehouse officer in their capacity as a team member and a future on-the-job trainer and recruitment officer. These select shortlisted candidates participated in a skills assessment workshop, followed by a face-to-face interview with set questions that were scored based on how well they answered. After this came psychometric and numeracy testing and a functional medical exam. The successful candidate was chosen as a result of her having achieved the highest scores across all activities. From my perspective, I cannot discriminate against an applicant who went to school with one of my children. Based on the size of my family, friends and professional network I experience one degree of separation between myself and anyone in my local area. If a relative or friend of mine had applied for the job, I would have declared the conflict of interest and removed myself from the process.

Because the female trainee was so scared of any repercussions and feared it would get worse than it already was, she did not want to lodge a formal complaint to HR about this bullying. So up until this point I had counselled the female trainee to rise above this treatment. And I spoke to both the old bully bloke and the female union member about how the trainee reflects how well we train them in the workplace, and I went through the list of behaviours of how to train a person well and how to treat young people appropriately in the workplace. This is when the female union member confided in me that she feared the old union rep, so she had to get along with him and be on good terms with him or she was worried she would be his target. She was unwilling to make a complaint about her workplace treatment by him, such as ignoring her, gossiping about her behind her back and refusing to help her with warehouse tasks. It was a case of 'if you can't beat him, join him.'

****

After a couple more weeks of juggling warehouse and supply teams, managing all the change that the implementation of a new corporation-wide system brought with it, I became so burnt out that I could not get out of bed one morning to go to work. When I went to deactivate my 5 am morning alarm, I found my hand was not functioning. I turned my bedside lamp on to find that my hand looked like it had exploded – it was swollen and looked like it was filled with blood. Off I went to my doctor's surgery to find out what was happening. The blood vessels in my hand had spontaneously ruptured causing bruising and the inability to move my fingers and use my hand. After a long discussion with my doctor, he prescribed a week off work to allow the blood to be reabsorbed into my body and advised that he could not cite any direct cause for the broken blood vessels, but suggested I needed to decrease the stress I was under at work.

Around this time, the commercial general manager that had supported me during the creation of the procure to pay system retired. He had worked for the Corporation for over a decade, and he told me he needed to spend more time with his wife and family. During the implementation of the system, he had brought the many non-compliance matters to the CEO's attention that had been discovered because of the systems application. The conflicts of interest, the many independent contractors in corporation positions, the owner drivers, the cultural awareness training being earmarked for an Aboriginal tribe selected by the human resources general manager (HR GM). At this point in time, my peer, the finance manager, stepped into the general manager position.

As I was sitting at home resting up for a week, the thought crossed my mind that when I first woke that morning to find my hand debilitated as it was full of blood, I thought I could have been having a stroke. I knew that I needed to pay attention to this sign; because sometimes your body tells you what your head is not. I returned to work and booked a meeting with the new acting commercial general manager (ACGM) to advise that I could no longer perform to two positions at the Corporation and that I needed to return to the warehouse, to one job immediately. Of course, he did not take this news well. I did think it would be a shock to him, but not only did he not take the news well, he questioned my mental stability and suggested I see the employee assistance programme counsellor. During this meeting, he also mentioned to me 'confidentially' that I needed to watch my back because the HR GM had put a target on it, because of the cultural awareness training bid process and how according to the HR GM my team had set her up for failure.

This new ACGM had no knowledge of the recently discovered commercial issues because he had not been involved in the creation and implementation of the new PTP system; and the non-compliance it had identified; including the HR GM's bias towards one Aboriginal tribe ahead of every other one. I knew I was on my own because this peer of mine had applied for the commercial GM position, so he was trying extremely hard to impress. I knew that if it meant 'taking me out' in the process, then it could occur. I went back to my old job in the warehouse and site services area, kept my head down and enjoyed returning home to my family before dark each night. I avoided the HR GM and the ACGM like the plague.

****

Corporate Storm

As I spent more time in the warehouse operation, I started to keep a closer eye on the treatment of the young female trainee, without the others knowing – there are a lot of places to stand hidden and observe between the aisles of materials. I, too, was starting to notice the inappropriate advances and actions the old union representative and his female union member were showing towards her. I started to pull them up for it because he was old enough to be her grandfather and she was old enough to be her mother. It astounded me how two people made a young person's life so difficult. But as I started to performance manage them, they turned up the heat further on the female trainee in an unexpected way. They started to spread a rumour that the female trainee was having a sexual affair with the oldest bloke in the warehouse team. The old union representative even referred to them as 'boyfriend and girlfriend' to customers and delivery drivers behind their backs. When the trainee and oldest team member found out what they had been saying, they confronted them one morning at pre-start and an escalated discussion started as the female trainee and the oldest team member held the two malicious gossipers responsible. However, because the female trainee was so worn down by the treatment, she fled the room crying. I had lost control of the meeting, so I ended it, and as I walked through the utility room, I discovered the old union rep had the trainee cornered, towering over her as she was in tears as he wanted to know what he had ever done to hurt her. I instantly slipped in front of the trainee and told her to go to my office and stood eyeball-to-eyeball with this bully. I could see the hate for me in his eyes and his face was bright red. I told him in a very calm, low voice – to keep away from her and get to work.

I then headed to the nearby toilet and vomited, before going to my office and advising the female trainee that either she lodged a formal complaint about her treatment, or I would. The trainee left work for the day to go to the doctor. She got a medical certificate and medication to calm her anxiety level and returned to work to lodge a formal written complaint with the Corporation's HR department.

THUNDER ROARS

In the meantime, I kept doing my job well by sticking to my daily routine, undertaking all the inspections and tasks that were expected of me. The rest of the team knew what was going on with the inappropriate treatment of the young female trainee and they were pleased that I had stood up for her with the two union bullies because they did not want to get picked on next. I also kept a remarkably close eye on the trainee to ensure that she was always separated from her two bullies while we waited for her bullying complaint to be progressed.

****

Weeks went by without anything changing – a lot of hovering going on for my part. A female trainee turning up for work each day waiting for an investigation to start. And I was going to a weekly meeting with the ACGM to talk about the warehouse operation and the people issues. During one of these weekly meetings the ACGM handed me a letter in an envelope. I opened it to find that it was a HR related letter on Corporation letterhead, signed by him and it Stated, 'Serious allegations have been made against me.' Nothing else. No information on what the claim was related to, who the claim was related to, timing for an investigation. Nothing. And when I asked for this information from the ACGM, he responded that it was confidential, and he was unable to advise. I left his office and booked an appointment with the employee assistance program counsellor to talk about *everything*.

Offloading everything to a counsellor was a huge relief. It was also nice to hear someone ask me how I was. The counsellor outlined that the behaviour at the Corporation was contradicting my personal values and was causing me stress. She suggested that we meet every fortnight. So, in my true-to-form, forward-planning style, we booked them into our calendars for the upcoming months.

****

Corporate Storm

I had a new female school-leaving Aboriginal trainee start in the warehouse team. She was bright-eyed, energetic and eager to learn. She formed a close working relationship with the existing female trainee, as there was only about 18 months' age difference. She worked well down the back of the warehouse with the team members in the receival bay and it was time for her to move to the front counter and serve customers. Her commencement on the front counter started on the Monday. She was working with the old union rep, so I kept checking in on her progress to make sure he had not started to treat her poorly. Anytime I sat back and observed the front counter I could see a lot of smiley faces and hear a lot of laughter, so it seemed like things were going well.

On the Thursday of the Aboriginal female trainee's first week on the front counter, it was National Reconciliation Week, so I arranged for her to go to the centralised crib rooms to help the other Aboriginal trainees and the Indigenous affairs team to set up for the ceremony and lunch. Not long after she had left the warehouse she returned to my office, arms crossed, shaking and in tears. I shut the door to find out what was wrong. She told me she had arrived on the veranda of the crib rooms and a union rep and his work mates were sitting at a crib room table and the union rep said something to her like, 'Aren't you going to get me my lunch for me? After all, you're the black fella.' She said she then turned around and she felt him touch her on the arse. She went onto say that is when she felt violated, and she headed back to my office. I sat with her, got her tissues and a drink of water and advised her that I needed to take her to HR so as she could report what had happened. She said she didn't want to because this was the union rep who had previously been hounding her to join the union and that him and the old union rep in the warehouse had been joking about how her arse looked similar to the female electrical apprentice's arse all week. It had been occurring since Monday, and she said the joke had worn thin and she didn't know how to tell him without him treating her like he did the other female trainee. I now understood that the two trainees had shared their personal workplace stories, as they had grown close. For the first time since starting at the Corporation I understood why the previous female warehouse employee (who had her breast groped) had said she felt like she'd been pimped out. It was being done again. I also realised that this pimping process was what all the smiling and laughter had been about in her first couple of days serving customers.

This was not a matter for a frontline leader to counsel a team member and write up a diary note. Even if it were only a verbal exchange by the harasser, I could not take matters into my hands as the harasser did not work for me. Aside from being limited by an organisational reporting structure, the harasser had overstepped the verbal boundary and actually touched the girl. I had a legal obligation to report this incident, even if the trainee did not. The workplace has a legal obligation to provide a safe place of work.

I told her that I had her back and that I was her protector and that we were going to walk down to the HR building. We would need to go past the centralised crib rooms but if we encountered anyone that had made her feel uncomfortable, she was to move herself behind my body and I would take care of the interaction. I assured her that she was safe with me and reminded her that as a mother of two daughters around the same age as her I was like a lioness protecting her cub. She smiled for a moment, but I knew she knew that I would look after her.

On the short walk to HR, it dawned on me that I needed to hand her over to the independent HR officer straight away so as I was not seen to be coercing her. The only reason this thought crossed my mind was because I was the only female leader in the business, and I already had a young female trainee with a HR complaint against a union rep and now I had another. I was the common denominator and an easy target for them to blame.

Once at HR, I handed her over to the HR manager while she briefly recounted what she had already told me. I then went to contact the Indigenous affairs co-ordinator to make sure that she had support and I returned to my office. By the time I got back to my desk the gossip had run wild and the warehouse team knew of the sexual harassment. I did not validate anything, but instead responded that it was a confidential HR matter and to not talk about it to maintain the privacy of the people involved. I was so angry about his foul interaction that I did my first ever impulsive behaviour as a leader – I walked over to the old union rep and said I need to speak to you in my office right now. I had not planned this interaction, but I wanted him to know that I was holding him responsible.

I called him into my office to sit down and I closed the door. I did not provide him any details of what had just happened; but I advised him confidentially that the Aboriginal trainee had just had a very unsettling encounter with some warehouse customers that was regarding a joke that he had been communicating at the front counter about her and the female electrical apprentice looking alike. He advised that he knew about the joke and that it had started on Monday, and he could tell by the afternoon that she was sick of the joke. Once he said that last part, I sat in my chair, reeling from my thoughts – this old bloke was such a bully that he lacked insight completely. Instead of getting angry at him and unveiling my deep negative judgement, I composed myself and asked him to act like a respectful father figure around the young female trainees, and to teach these young ladies straight out of school the workplace boundaries and to help them not to accept any behaviour that makes them feel uncomfortable. I asked him to pull anyone up that oversteps the mark and takes a joke too far, continue a joke too long or even jokes at someone else's expense. I requested that he help make the young female trainees feel comfortable in the workplace. He assured me that he would, and he returned to work.

The Aboriginal trainee did not return to work that day.

Thunder Roars

****

Early the following morning I received a phone call from the HR manager wanting to know if the Aboriginal trainee had arrived at work. She was at work, and I was keeping a close eye on her because she described to me that she had not slept, she was scared, nervous and had diarrhoea. The HR manager asked me to advise him once again what had happened yesterday afternoon. So, I recounted the story again. He then said he was concerned that I would be targeted by the union for coercion because it was a trainee making a complaint against a union rep. I responded that was why I had taken her to HR straight away because I aware of the severity of the complaint and I did not want to be seen as coercing her lodge a complaint; but that it did not matter anyway; because the moment she said she felt violated the Corporation had a legal responsibility under the Workplace Health and Safety legislation to take action. So even if she did not lodge a formal complaint the Corporation needed to have a discussion with this union rep to counsel him that these actions were illegal, inappropriate and will not be accepted in this place of work. In addition, I recommended that personal development training should be scheduled for the union rep in understanding equal employment opportunity, harassment, bulling and discrimination and diversity and how these factors affect a workplace. I advised that I was willing to be involved in the discussion with the union rep so as he would understand how much his actions had negatively affected a new employee in the workforce, straight out of high school.

The HR manager said that he would not be doing anything; because when he previously stood up against the union it almost cost him his job and the malicious rumours that generated created a lot of stress on his family because they were about him being the next target to be sacked. He said I needed to be careful because the union would lodge counterclaims against me. I was furious and told him that he needed to act because this trainee was around the same age as his daughter and young women deserve better. I said that if he were unwilling to take action, I would. I told him that I was going to escalate this matter to the CEO because from the CEO presentations I had attended he seemed like a family man with a young adult daughter that he spoke fondly of, and he seemed to be a leader, and if I had to go so far as the Chairman of the Board to achieve the right outcome for this Aboriginal trainee then I would. I had seen the Chairman across many years at public events treat his wife like a good, respectful, devoted husband, and he had always greeted me and my daughters respectfully. I told the HR manager that I could not allow for this matter to be swept under the rug, so if I had to escalate it for it to be managed properly then I would. The HR manager only responded with, 'Well, don't throw me under the bus when you get there.' I did not have to throw him under any bus because the fact that he did nothing just left him as roadkill in the events to come.

****

To make matters worse for my highly affected Aboriginal trainee, the union rep couldn't abide by the confidentiality clause of any HR related matter and he was overheard boasting to the other workshop team members that he'd pinched the Aboriginal trainee on the arse the other day, and he'd been to see the Chairman of the Board to find out what could go on and been told that the most that would happen is that he'd be stood down on full pay while an investigation was undertaken and then he'd give a teary apology and it would all be over. This got back to the trainee and I with a warning that if we pursued an investigation, we would be targets of the union.

An investigation was started by the HR GM, and not an independent investigator as is normally required of serious HR related matters. In the meantime, I organised for the Aboriginal trainee to be transferred to another department to continue her traineeship, and I relocated the other female trainee out of the warehouse team to the supply team where she could finish her traineeship.

Once I had finished finalising these arrangements, I was contacted by the ACGM to attend a meeting with him to discuss a serious HR matter. Over the telephone I asked if this were finally an investigation into the treatment of the trainees could we meet today; instead of continuing to drag things out. I also asked if by the end of the meeting an investigation could be under way, and I could be stood down instead of hovering around the workplace worried about how people are being inappropriately treated. To which he responded, 'Yes,' and committed to meet with me a couple of hours later.

I calmly packed up my desk, diaries, supporting evidence from the HR matters and non-compliance from implementing the procure to pay system and I took it all home. I arranged for my husband to accompany me back to work to this special meeting.

'It is better to have less thunder in the mouth and more lightening in the hand.'
Apache, Native American tribe

CHAPTER 4

Lightning Strikes

'Be the lightning bolt in the room. The person with explosive energy that touches everyone.'
Elle Smith

Before walking into the meeting, I advised my husband that he would be my support person, to sit quietly and if he needed to speak with me as a matter of priority in the meeting, then to ask to pull me to one side. I told him that no matter what happened in the meeting, he needed to allow me to handle it and not make any strange faces or tell-tale body language, and if things got tricky in the meeting, I said that I like to rely on awkward silence as a strategy, so please do not break it. I had prepared him that this meeting was finally what I had been waiting for and was the culmination of the past six months of two female trainees' matters not being taken seriously and the serious allegations raised against me by the union as counterclaims without substance to silence me. I arrived in the meeting thinking I was finally going to be stood aside on full pay for the HR investigation process to be followed properly for these trainees. The meeting interaction went something like this:

- **Acting commercial general manager (ACGM)** – *Advised that the issues in the warehouse team are continuing to be pursued and he's understood that I wish to keep my good reputation intact, and he's noticed the issues have taken a toll on my health and how I feel about these issues. The Corporation are willing to pay me out much more than anyone else has ever been paid out to leave the Corporation.*
- **Me** – *Advised that the safety and operational performance of the warehouse was brilliant, the rest of the team other than two people are really good, productive team members.*
- **ACGM** – *Advised that I had made my feelings very clear on the emails and many communications I'd had with him. And they were going to pay me six months' salary and I'd sign a waiver and confidentiality agreement upon departure.*
- **Me** – *Asked if there were any other options.*
- **ACGM** – *Due to a loss of faith with the warehouse team the warehouse position was no longer an option and they'd considered special projects but really there was nothing available.*
- **Me** – *Asked whether I had anything in writing for him.*
- **ACGM** – *No. Actual figures would have to be worked out later. What are my initial thoughts?*
- **Me** – *So, you're paying me to go away?*
- **ACGM** – *Yes.*
- **Me** – *Asked if the CEO knows about this.*
- **ACGM** – *Responded that it's an authorised offer.*
- *Awkward silence...*
- **ACGM** – *Advised that he would phone me tomorrow to see how I was feeling.*
- **Me** – *Placed my Corporation vehicle keys and electronic access badge on the table.*
- **ACGM** – *Asked if the vehicle was parked in the Corporation car park.*
- **Me** – *Yes.*

Lightning Strikes

When I arrived home 20 minutes later, I tried to log into the Corporation's computer network to create a polite out of office email to direct people towards the ACGMs because I was away from the workplace, to find I had been locked out of the computer network already.

After being floored by this conversation and removal of all Corporation accesses it effectively equated to termination without anything in writing, so I contacted an employment lawyer seeking legal advice.

****

I covered all the workplace matters with the employment lawyer over several telephone calls. I then scanned and emailed all the supporting evidence for the HR matters and noncompliance from implementing the procure to pay system to inform him of everything I had stood up for. He was so interested in the matter that he arranged for me to meet with himself and a barrister in Brisbane to discuss options within days.

After meeting with me they advised that unless I had been terminated there was not much they could do as legal action on my behalf. However, after they witnessed my professional approach and capability, they recommended that I escalate not only the treatment of the female trainees to the CEO, but also my clumsy treatment by the ACGM. They suggested that instead of them sending a legal letter to the CEO on my behalf that I appeared capable and resilient enough to continue to represent myself, keep it in-house by taking my husband as support person and arrange a meeting with the CEO to allow him to do the right thing on behalf of the Corporation.

I sent the CEO an email to arrange a meeting and provided him a summary of the sequence of events to date, which included me providing a summarised version of the HR matters and noncompliance from implementing the procure to pay system and advising him that I had the supporting evidence if he wished to see it. I outlined in the letter that from my discussions with an employment lawyer I understood I had three options.

1. Make a legal claim that encompasses the following:
    a. I had only positive performance review documents and had never been performance managed for being an ineffective leader throughout these multiple HR matters. But I had been instructed and warned to take a hands-off approach in these HR matters because the people involved were union reps and members.
    b. The malicious intent of the unfounded serious allegations that were raised against me as reprisal action, no scope, no timeline, no investigation interview for myself at any time.
    c. The medical and psychological records proving the negative affect on my personal health due to teenage girls being sexually harassed and bullied and no investigation.
    d. The overall lack of procedural fairness and mismanagement by the Corporation of the matters surrounding myself.
2. Take the hush money, sign the deed of confidentiality and waiver to act and walk away.
3. Reassign me in the organisation to develop and implement the many other management systems that need to be created, such as contract management, contractor management, project management, customer management, etc.

****

The CEO met with me within days. At no stage during the meeting did he ask to view any evidence or commit to investigate anything. I sat there and left lots of awkward silence. The meeting interaction went something like this:

- **CEO** – *Welcomed me into his office to sit at his round conference table.*
- **CEO** – *Once seated, he said, 'Well, I got your email you've sent me, so you tell me?' as he stared directly at me the entire conversation.*
- **Me** – *I outlined in summary the contents of the email I'd previously provided as preparation for this meeting; with regards the HR matters and himself and the Board had asked me to develop and implement a procure to pay system that had uncovered people's non-compliance like the list of issues contained in my email. I highlighted that the Corporation had a sick culture where young women are treated inappropriately and when the 18-year-old Indigenous trainee was touched on the bottom by the union representative it made me feel sick. 'I view these girls as if they are my own daughters because they are of similar age and I wouldn't want my daughters working at this Corporation.'*
- **Me** – *I went onto say that I was shocked with the offer last week by the ACGM of hush money to leave the organisation, when I thought I was being invited to a meeting to finally discuss the ongoing bullying and harassment of female trainees by union reps and members. These serious HR matters have been unresolved for six months. 'It's just worn me down, so I was ready to be stood aside while people's inappropriate behaviour was finally investigated. I've been hovering for months watching over these young women making sure people old enough to be their parents or grandparents don't treat them badly.' I went onto to look him directly in the eye, pointed my finger and said, 'As CEO, you are responsible for the organisation's culture. I want young women to be able to come to work here and feel safe.'*
- *Awkward silence…*
- **CEO** – *Advised that, 'You have two options: option A – stay as the leader of the warehouse and site services team, or option B*

- *a payout to be calculated and that's not a job that I do; so, the payout would be negotiated and calculated later.'*
- **Me** – Said, *'I feel like I'm being sacrificed and paid hush money to walk away instead of handling the people issues and resolving the problems. And that option A was not even on offer by ACGM last week.'*
- **CEO** – *'I had heard you have been seeking employment externally.'*
- **Me** – *'No I haven't applied for any jobs. In fact I've been approached for opportunities in other businesses, but I don't want to leave until all these matters are settled. I don't want to leave the girls on their own.'*
- **CEO** – Responded, *'The ACGM had been clumsy is how he communicated it because he's not used to doing this kind of conversation. But that the ACGM had come to him and said things are getting really messy in the warehouse and there are lots of claims, counterclaims and Jen is getting very stressed out. I took that on-board because he said it was affecting your health and your home life so I said if it were for the best, he could make an offer for a payout.'*
- **Me** – Reiterated that, *'Last week returning to my job was not even offered by the ACGM, but now I understand it is an option.'*
- **CEO** – *'Yes, it's an option, and if you decide to return to your position there will be a messy investigation with lots of gossip and rumours that can't be controlled that could ruin your reputation.'* At this point he looked across at my husband and said, *'You've been a long-term employee of the Corporation and you know what this place is like with gossip.'* He then turned his focus back to me and said, *'A lengthy investigation and time away from work can create more stress on yourself and your home life. The ACGM has previously covered the issues raised against you.'*

- **Me** – *Responded, 'Yes, the ACGM has previously covered issues with me in general without any definitive information or supporting evidence. I have never been interviewed for any allegations. I have no idea of what the content of these issues is about, and they have been going for the past six months and have remained unresolved. I feel the organisation asked me to design and implement a Procure to Pay System to create compliance and end the business' flexibility and optionality and then when I've discovered the non-compliance, you're not resolving it; instead, you're sacrificing me and getting rid of me. Since the implementation of PTP I've felt completely unsupported, and I understand I am seen as rigid across the organisation and that I have stood on people's toes in the implementation process; however, it was my responsibility to ensure same or I'd be exposed for not doing my job legally. And then with the poor behaviour towards people, I've done everything the organisation has asked of me – I've been going to your employee assistance program counsellor, and I've been seeing my doctor. Employees' HR claims aren't being treated seriously nor progressed independently, and a bogus claim has been made against me that I have no idea of the content and I've never been asked to meet to discuss it with anyone.'*
- **CEO** – *Stated, 'Well, you need to make a decision option A or option B and please let the ACGM of your decision.'*
- **Me** – *'So, that's it, option A or B – there's no other option? Even though the Corporation is still not compliant to the Government Procurement Policy and the new procure to pay system needs to be developed to encompass this Government Policy. On top of this the Corporation has so many other systems to be developed that I am experienced in.'*
- **CEO** – *Said, 'I don't like moving people around the organisation because the issues just don't go away by themselves. You seem*

to be the common person involved in the people issues. The only way people leave the organisation is by positive drug and alcohol results and you're being offered a payout to leave.'
- **Me** – Responded, 'Yes, I am the common denominator because the people issues exist and I don't leave them go unnoticed. And people are able to get away with inappropriate behaviour because no one is held responsible, and nothing progresses. I know I've upset the people that do the wrong thing and now they dislike me. They're making claims against me, and I'm not informed or invited to participate in an investigation or resolution. I feel completely unsupported as a leader by this organisation. There is never any resolution.'
- Awkward silence...
- **CEO** – Advised, 'As described, you've got option A or option B. If we need to pay you for another couple of weeks for you to decide then I'm willing to do that.'
- Longer awkward silence.
- **Me** – Thanked him for his time and committed I'd contact the ACGM the following week to advise of my choice.

Lightning Strikes

My husband and I left the CEO's office and walked out of the corporate building in silence. We hopped into our car and before starting it, I turned to him and asked, 'Do I have your support no matter how hard things may get?' Of course, he responded, 'Yes.' I went onto tell him, 'That was like waving a red rag in front of a bull. Talk about a bully. He was not interested in understanding anything. He just wants the little woman that is making things difficult for people to go away.' My husband joked, 'Yes – get back into the kitchen!'

'Lighting makes no sound until it strikes.'
Martin Luther King Jnr

CHAPTER 5

Cyclonic Winds Blow

'When the winds of change blow, some people build walls and others build windmills.'
Rishika Jains

As I had committed myself to doing, the following week I sent an email to the ACGM to decline the Corporation's hush money – the payout sum that was yet to be negotiated and if I needed more time to consider taking it then the CEO was willing to pay for longer to decide. Because I was not willing to turn my back and walk away on the inappropriate treatment of two female trainees, and now my treatment was described as clumsy, but now I had discovered the true lengths a bully Executive will go to.

The following day after declining the offer of the hush money; instead of an investigation into the girls or my treatment commencing, I received another letter from the ACGM of the Corporation to advise me that more serious claims had been raised against me. Nothing else. No information on what the claim was related to, who the claim was related to, timing for an investigation. Nothing. Another intimidation tactic in the hope that I would go away.

Remember that I originally walked out of the first hush money offer meeting. So, I technically stood myself aside from the workplace on full pay. Two weeks passed, and I was informed in this letter of a second set of serious allegations raised against me and the letter also advised me that I was now stood aside by the Corporation on full pay.

Private and Confidential

By email

Dear Jennifer,

Response to Correspondence... Notice to Stand Aside

I refer to a recent conversation involving yourself, your partner Joe McGuire and the CEO... whereby discussions occurred regarding your role at the Corporation.

Following that meeting, I note your email correspondence of...whereby you expressed your intent to participate in any investigation process undertaken by the Corporation.

As discussed during your meeting with the CEO, the Corporation has become aware of a number of matters pertaining to yourself, by way of formal allegations. The Corporation has serious concerns regarding these allegations, and will now undertake a process to explore the validity of the information provided.

Whilst the Corporation works through these matters, you will be stood aside, effective immediately. Your standing aside will continue until matters are finalised unless you are otherwise instructed by me. You will continue to receive your normal salary during this time.

From receiving this notification, you are instructed to refrain from attending the workplace unless otherwise directed by the Corporation. Nor shall you contact any other employee, suppliers or customers of the Corporation, except your employee representative, without the Corporation's consent. The Corporation will be in contact with you in the short term to advise of next steps regarding any investigation process to be undertaken.

It is the Corporation's expectation that whilst you are stood aside, that you will be available within 24-hours' notice to attend any meetings scheduled on a normal working day...

Regards...

At this point I knew the Executive did not want me to return to the workplace, they were either going to bully me into taking the hush money or intimidate me until I resigned. I was also worried for my husband of 20-plus years because I was likening this process to childbirth. As in, he is there as my solid support but is helpless because he cannot put me out of my pain. In addition, during childbirth the husband has the unknown of how much pain you are really in. Could she have waited longer for pain medication? Could she have waited longer before pushing? Here my husband was wondering by now, 'Could the Corporation make up claims about my wife? Could the Corporation ruin my wife's professional reputation?' At no time did he ever lose faith in me delivering one of our babies, and so he never lost faith in me taking on the Corporation's administration for their mismanagement.

The unexpected aspect for the Corporation's Executive was that they had targeted a person that was not fearful of keeping a job. At this point,

I had a successful career spanning over 25 years. I had always been the women in leadership roles pioneer. Usually the only woman in a non-traditional leadership position. A part of the 4 per cent female on an industrial site. I had been the person that wrote business cases and policy for equal employment opportunity, parental leave, subsidised childcare and a breastfeeding room for new working mums in other organisations. I knew that I had previously been registered globally as international management talent for a multinational Corporation. I had previously won Australian Institute of Management awards that are all voted on by peers and team members. I knew that I had encountered an Executive whose workplace values did not meet my expectation and I was not going to run away. I was going to hold them responsible for their actions and I knew that I would not get anyone terminated; but I was going to make them feel uncomfortable, lay awake at night and trigger them to have some insight into why a woman would stand up and fight so hard and not reap any benefit for themselves.

The next day I received a phone call from the ACGM to ask if I had received their letter and how I was feeling about it. I kept the telephone call short and did not provide him any information about how I was feeling or what I was thinking. From this point forward I knew what I had to do, and I was not about to ruin it by telling anyone. I asked him about what was the nature of the serious claims that had been raised against me, who had raised them and what was the forecast timing of the investigation. The most information I got out of him was a statement that the investigation is confidential, and he was unable to provide any details. A desktop review of the information was being undertaken this week. I asked when I would be interviewed. And he told me within two weeks.

The two weeks flew by. It gave me the opportunity to completely itemise all the evidence I had removed from my office. I categorised it multiple ways – against my diary notes and similar events – so I was ready to meet with any independent investigator. Unfortunately, I never received a phone call or email inviting me anywhere to discuss anything concerning the Corporation. So, after work hours I sent a text to the Chairman of the Board outlining my matter. I sent him this text after hours because I wanted to give him the opportunity of keeping everything in house and resolving the matter.

Text message to the Chairman of the Corporation Board:

Hello Chairman,

I am wishing to meet with you for a private discussion or send you an email to your personal address privately to advise the clumsy handling of the issues relating to myself & the 2 teenage female trainees in the warehouse team. The gossip has continued & I'm concerned with a federal election approaching & your union reps quoting your involvement in their protection. I have met with the CEO & was diverted back to the ACGM so the investigation and resolution of the many issues is taking too long, so hence the gossip is manifesting & I'm concerned someone is going to leak to the media. I've been offered 'hush' money to walk away but I've been stressed for months taking care of these young ladies in the workplace. I've also highlighted that I have experience in systems development & economic development & could be relocated within the business. If no action is taken I will return to work after this protracted messy investigation & continue to counter the poor behaviour of the union reps/members that sexually harass & bully young females. Please let me know how you wish to proceed.

Regards, Jennifer McGuire

Corporate Storm

Text message from the Chairman of the Corporation Board:

Jennifer.

Thank you for contacting me. You text message has raised matters of serious concern. You have made several serious allegations with respect to your treatment and to the behaviour of a group of employees of the Corporation.

The first is that the handling of issues relating to your employment and two female trainees has been clumsy.

The second is that union reps/members are quoting my involvement in their protection.

The third is that the investigation and resolution of the many issues is taking too long.

The fourth is that you have been offered 'hush' money to walk away.

The fifth is that on your return to work you will continue to counter the poor behaviour of union reps/members that sexually harass and bully young females.

Employment matters are the domain of the CEO who is charged with running the organisation. However, you have now raised very serious allegations of violation of the policies and procedures of the Corporation and as Chairman I am duty bound to refer them to the Board of the Corporation.

The usual procedure for the Board in such matters is to directly engage an independent highly qualified professional to review all matters relating to the issues you have raised and any others you may wish to raise prior to the investigation taking place.

I will seek the Board's support for this course of action early next week so there is no further delay in the investigation of the matter you have raised.

Jennifer, the Federal election is immaterial in the extreme.

My duty and role as Chairman is to oversee the lawful and professional conduct of the Corporation in accordance with the laws governing the Corporation and the policies and procedures of the Corporation.

The contents of your text message and of my response will be submitted to the Board.

Again, thank you for contacting me. Chairman of the Corporation Board.

Text message to the Chairman of the Corporation Board:

Many thanks Chairman. I have all the supporting materials & have consulted an employment lawyer. It is the lawyer who suggested that I ensure that you were aware of the prolonged clumsy handling.

I was ultimately pleased that the Chairman undertook the legally compliant action that the employment lawyer had explained was his duty. I was finally going to have the independent investigation the girls deserved and that I now needed.

Within days, I had a telephone call from the Corporation's company secretary. She explained that she had been tasked by the Board to arrange a Board-appointed independent investigator to investigate my claims in accordance with the Crime Corruption Commission process.

Once I heard the CCC term, I knew that I was now in a situation that I had no prior experience for, so in my normal workplace behaviour, I did some research. This made me understand the positive aspect of being protected under the whistleblower legislation for escalating my issues with the Corporation's administration, as per the following:

> Public interest disclosures (whistleblowing)
>
> Providing information about wrongdoing in the public sector is commonly known as 'whistleblowing'. The legal term for it is 'making a public interest disclosure (PID)'. PIDs about corruption can be made to the **CCC**. In **Queensland**, public sector employees who disclose information as a result of genuine concern about possible corruption in the public sector are protected by law (the *Public Interest Disclosure Act 2010*) from reprisals.

My internet research also made me understand that if the investigator thought my issues lacked substance or credibility, or were frivolous, vexatious or malicious and not made in good faith then an investigation would be waste of public resources and to deal with the matter could not be further justified and my issues would be referred right back to the Corporation administration where I had just been intimidated.

The following week, I was in a motel conference room sitting in front of an investigator and being advised of all the CCC process, policy and how the interview method would be undertaken. I was advised of the confidentiality requirements, how the interview audio would be recorded and once typed up I could access the record to ensure accuracy. It was explained to me that this first meeting was to determine if my claim was valid for an investigation to occur.

Five hours later, the investigator turned the recording device off, leant over the table and advised me that I was the most organised, succinct person she had ever interviewed. I responded that I had waited over six months for the inappropriate treatment of the first female trainee to be investigated, then the independent investigation of the Aboriginal trainee and then the mismanagement of me. I had finally received what I had been asking for – an investigation. I no longer felt like I was fighting. I had finally been heard. This is when I burst into tears for the first time. They were tears of relief because I had recounted the entire story to the investigator, and she took a courier bag full of supporting evidence, including my four workplace diaries. I could do no more.

The occurrence of the CCC investigation was covered in newspapers.

THE OBSERVER

Saturday, August 18, 2018

Andrew Thorpe

UPDATE: GPC remains tight-lipped on Zussino's role

Leo Zussino speaks at the GAPDL Cruise Business Luncheon 2018. Matt Taylor GLA120618GAPDL

SUNDAY, 5.30PM: Gladstone Ports Corporation has refused to confirm if chairman Leo Zussino has stood aside after a complaint about how the business was run was referred to the Crime and Corruption Commission.

It is not suggested the claims in the complaint - which are yet to be assessed - relate directly to Mr Zussino's conduct.

Speaking to the media after the Botanic to Bridge run today, GPC chief executive Peter O'Sullivan remained tight-lipped when asked about Mr Zussino's current role.

"We don't have any full details about the issue or the individuals involved," he said.

"It would be inappropriate to make further comment."

Mr O'Sullivan repeated his statement yesterday that the company would cooperate with the CCC and described the process as an example of "good governance".

Former GPC chief executive Craig Doyle heard about the complaint yesterday.

Mr Doyle held the position from September 2013 to January 2016.

He is now the chief executive at Mackay Regional Council.

"I had no concerns with how the business was run during my time at GPC," he said.

Member for Gladstone Glenn Butcher said he understood the Gladstone Ports Corporation board met this afternoon to discuss the CCC assessment.

While he could not confirm if the chairman had stood aside, Mr Butcher said it was a normal process for the person in charge of an organisation to take leave while a CCC assessment was taking place.

"I'm sure GPC has done its due diligence and they will work very closely with the CCC," Mr Butcher said.

A CCC spokesman said it was important to note an assessment was not an investigation.

"When the CCC receives a complaint, it first conducts an assessment to determine whether the matter falls within the CCC's jurisdiction, whether an investigation is warranted, and, if so, which agency should be responsible," the spokesman said.

Mr Zussino has contacted The Observer and said previous stories about the CCC assessment were inaccurate, but did not respond to further questions.

Gladstone's port is Queensland's largest multi-commodity port.
CHRISSY HARRIS

6.50PM: Gladstone Ports Corporation chairman Leo Zussino has stood aside following a complaint to the state's crime watchdog about GPC's administration, according to the Sunday Mail.

It is understood Mr Zussino stood aside on Friday afternoon.

It is not suggested the claims in the complaint - which are yet to be assessed - relate directly to Mr Zussino's conduct.

Mr Zussino, 70, has been associated with the port for almost three decades, helping to develop it into Queensland's largest multi-commodity port.

He previously served as the then-Gladstone Port Authority's chairman from 1990 to 1999, before being appointed chief executive in 2000.

He was fired from the position by the Newman Government in 2013, before being appointed chairman once again in 2015.

Mr Zussino is also the namesake of the main building on CQUniversity's Gladstone Marina campus.

He was unable to be contacted for comment by News Corp this evening.

A GPC board member contacted by The Observer said he was not in a position to comment.

Gladstone Ports Corporation also runs operations in Bundaberg and Rockhampton.

6.11PM: GLADSTONE Ports Corporation has released a statement from chief executive Peter O'Sullivan in response to yesterday's referral of a complaint about the running of the organisation to the Crime and Corruption Commission.

"Gladstone Ports Corporation is aware that concerns have been brought to the attention of our shareholding Ministers and that the Under Treasurer has subsequently referred these matters to the Crime and Corruption Commission," Mr O'Sullivan said.

"GPC is committed to cooperating fully with the CCC during its investigation.

"However, as the matter is now before the CCC, it is inappropriate to comment further."

4.14PM: THE STATE Government has referred a complaint "raising concerns about administration" at the Gladstone Ports Corporation to the Crime and Corruption Commission.

A joint statement from Treasurer Jackie Trad and Transport Minister Mark Bailey said the information was recently brought to the attention of GPC shareholding ministers, who reported it to the Queensland Treasury.

Under Treasurer Jim Murphy referred the matter to the Crime and Corruption Commission late yesterday.

"As the matter is before the CCC it is inappropriate to comment further," the statement read.

'Be the wind to drive others. A leaf which falls from the tree is at the mercy of wind. It goes wherever wind takes it... be the wind to drive others, not the leaf to be driven by others.'
Rishika Jains

CHAPTER 6

The Eye of the Storm

*'Serenity is not freedom from the storm
but peace amid the storm.'*
Adrian Rogers

I spent many weeks at home, laying low, not talking to anyone because I could not trust that they would not breach confidentiality and impart the events inaccurately. It was a challenging time, because our family of four is a part of an even bigger, local family, and my husband and I volunteer in many different not-for-profit and sporting organisations. Rumours were rife with some commentary that resembled the truth, but mostly it was about me being terminated. I had been sacked and marched out by the HR GM. I had been provided a large payout to leave. It was not until the CCC investigation into the Corporation's administration was covered very generally in the media that some people drew the connection.

It was so important for me to keep my mouth shut, that when interacting with people around sports grounds and social functions I had to make sure that I never provided any detail or got involved in any workplace-related conversations. I am testament to the fact that there are so many other topics to talk about other than work. People would ask how I was, and I would tell them I was doing 'really well, thanks. If people asked if I was still at the Corporation, I would answer that I was. If Corporation employees asked why they had not seen me at the Corporation for a while I would tell them I was on paid leave. If anyone ever pressed further and asked what is going on I have heard you are sticking up for those girls' treatment, or something similar, I would respond that I was the complainant for a confidential CCC investigation into the Corporation's administration and that I did not want to talk about it in case it ruined the integrity of the process. I never had a single person ask me anything after I would tell them that.

I spent three months at home occupying myself mostly within my home – cooking, gardening, reading many inspirational books about other whistleblower and pioneering tales. I had never previously had time to download a podcast and listen; but I took advantage of the downtime to catch up on what I had been missing out on. My husband and I do not watch a lot of television because I would usually be walking in the door from work at 6 pm at night. However, seeing he is a shift worker we started to watch a Netflix series together. Some of the recreational activities that other people participate in were a part of our home life, as I waited for the investigation to be over and to be invited back to work. I had found a way of accepting my new boring normal, waiting patiently and having faith in the process until...

****

At 4pm on 4 September 2018, I received a panicked phone call from one of my older daughters, Eliza. My youngest 13-year-old twin son, Harrison, had fallen off his bicycle and was lying on the ground waiting for the ambulance to arrive. I drove to the accident site and followed the ambulance into the bush to find Harrison lying on the dirt, skin scraped off him. His twin brother, Frazer, had kept him still, poured his water bottle contents on his scrapes and phoned his sisters. His sisters had rushed to the accident site. I was on the phone and their father asleep on nightshift, so they fortunately used their instinct and did not wait for any parental instructions and instead raised the emergency alarm.

I crouched down over him lying still on the dirt and picked up both of his hands. His older sister, Annaliese, who is a dental nurse, said to me that his teeth were okay and had been holding his head and neck still at the accident site since she had arrived and phoned the ambulance. He did not move; but he whispered, 'I can't feel anything.' I said, 'I've got a hold of your hands,' and he responded, 'I can't feel it.'

The ambulance officers asked if they could cut his clothing off. I told them to do whatever they needed to and got up and walked away to give them room. The three kids and I moved away. I went to the back of my car and threw up; because I knew that this was major. The girls wanted to know what to do about letting their dad know because he was asleep. I instructed Eliza to go and wake her father and drive him to the crash site and Annaliese to stay and not leave Frazer unattended at any time; because I knew he had seen what happened, he would be the first to feel the emotion and I knew that I needed to focus on Harrison.

Annaliese stayed with Frazer while Eliza drove home to get Joe. While this was happening, I went over and sat with Harrison as the ambulance officers went through their observations. Once the school shirt was removed you could see a massive red patch all over his neck and down onto his chest. The ambulance officer asked me if he had been sunburnt recently. No, he had not. It was like seeing all the blood had rushed to the neck and chest of his body and was overwhelming the area. He was beginning to groan in pain and the green whistle was doing nothing. The ambulance officers put his head in between two sandbags and strapped his forehead to become immobilised.

I looked up to see Eliza returning with Joe and saw that spectators had started to gather. Some kids in school uniforms and a father had walked into the vacant block. I just saw red at the ambulance watchers. I walked over to see them, and I asked to speak to the father figure. I just said to him that I did not appreciate by-standers at what is the worst time of my son's young life. He said that a couple of the boys had been bike riding with Harrison and Frazer when the accident happened, so I said I would be in contact and asked that they not stand around because I felt things were so serious for him that he could die there on the dirt.

I turned back around to meet Joe as he got out of the car to assess the situation for himself. He crouched down over Harrison and said, 'It's okay mate, it's probably just a broken collarbone.'

I know that Joe is the worrier of our family, so when it was time for the ambulance to leave, I told him to ride with Harrison. Going through the motions of getting everyone organised as to who was going where with who, Joe just kept on saying things like, 'It could be two broken collarbones, it will all be okay.' I pulled him to one side and told him to be prepared for the worst; because from what I could see from the impact point on his bike helmet, the blood rushing to his neck and chest and him not feeling our hand-holding that it could be more major. Joe was still half asleep and not quite all-there. The best decision was to have him ride with the ambos in case he went into shock. The rest of us went home with the bicycles and caught up with the ambulance as it had pulled over on the side of the road on the way to the hospital to be intercepted by another ambulance carrying a medic to meet Harrison, who was struggling to survive. He was struggling to breathe on the short ride and a medic came out to install an intravenous drip for the distribution of life-saving medications. Joe leapt out of the front seat of the ambulance and buckled over – the reality had just hit him; he had realised it was not a simple broken collarbone.

The Eye of the Storm

We continued our journey to the hospital where the nurses and doctors advised that our regional hospital was not equipped for any types of serious injuries, and they were sending him for medical images straight away.

Within moments, the outcome was as bad as I was thinking and much worse than Joe had ever thought – he had broken his C2 spinal vertebra, and it was a very unstable 45-degree angle break. Not that there is an easy way to break your neck; but the doctors explained that they had no idea how he had survived, and the angle of the break created a large surface area to try to repair and heal. The doctors explained that the regional hospital did not have any lifesaving medications or pain killers for Harrison's serious injury. Harrison could simply die by choking on his own saliva. They said they had been in consultation with the neurological spinal team at a Brisbane Hospital, they were expecting him and the rescue flight with the spinal injury retrieval team were on their way. This injury was so serious that Harrison was not waiting in a priority queue to be evacuated. Harrison was the biggest priority in the State and the team would arrive as soon as they could.

Over the next couple of hours, we just took it in turns, cycling in and out of Harrison's emergency bed side. Based on the skills, equipment and pain killers the regional hospital could provide Harrison's pain level never got any better than 9 out of 10. He was in agony; but the doctors could not risk him have a reaction to any medications. His body had to remain completely still. I am usually the family member that shows no emotion. I am a thinker. I process, process and process information. I am the family member that organises, plans everything, identifies solutions and is the rock that everyone else can depend upon during life's struggles. This time, I was an emotional wreck, and I did not want Harrison to see his strong mother crying because then he would know how dire a situation, he was in.

Once the spinal retrieval team arrived, the head doctor spoke to Joe and I and advised that they had all the specialist spinal injury medications to give him and asked who was going to accompany him on the emergency flight. That was Joe.

Once the emergency flight left, we went home and got organised for having a displaced household. I asked the kids if they wanted to come to Brisbane too; but Eliza was studying university externally, Annaliese worked fulltime, Frazer did not want to sit at a hospital and hospitals are not a comfortable place to be at any time. I stayed up all night getting organised and had a very relieved telephone conversation with Joe at 2 am when the Brisbane Hospital spinal team had evaluated Harrison and said that he would not die. Relief. So, I laid on the bed and tossed and turned until daylight when I would drive to Brisbane.

I stopped halfway to get a cup of tea and have a leg stretch and when I went to drive off in our Landcruiser, I found that it would not start. I phoned roadside service and they could not get me restarted again. I had a choice – either being towed to Brisbane and they would park the Landcruiser under the Brisbane Hospital for me to deal with it there; or they could take me home. Based on family connections in mechanical businesses at home I chose to make the long trip back. At first, I was upset that I could not get to Harrison that day, but sometimes the universe throws you a life rope. On the tow truck trip back to home, the driver was a retired paramedic. He had retired because he had seen too many horrific road crash scenes. The best part about the trip home was the conversation and how he asked me many questions to step him through what had happened, and he explained to me what the ambulance officers, medic, doctors and spinal retrieval team had done. He put my mind at rest.

My brother-in-law's workshop discovered I was so distracted that I had placed unleaded fuel into the Landcruiser instead of diesel. While my brother-in-law worked late to remove the fuel from the tank and change filters to restart the car. I ate dinner supplied by kind friends and enjoyed the company of my three other children. I had a better night sleep and got on the road the following day to see my son.

During my drive to Brisbane, Harrison was placed in an appliance called a screwless halo brace to prevent any movement of his head, neck or chest. He was, and still is, in massive amounts of pain, despite being on the strongest painkillers. He was in too much pain to talk or eat. However, lying on the bed he could move his limbs and was getting some strange sensations throughout his body.

Across the next four days of sitting bedside vigil, I started to notice that his head and face were twisting up, like a person with cerebral palsy. This was not a good sign. On day five after his accident, the pain management team arrived at Harrison's bedside and talked to Joe and I across the bed like he wasn't even laying there. These three doctors advised that Harrison was in severe pain fulltime and even the strong painkillers were no longer managing it and that we needed to consent to put him onto a nerve-blocker. I asked what a nerve-blocker would do, and they explained that it would block the pain messages from the damaged nerves to the brain so as he would be more comfortable. They explained that third-degree burns patients and serious spinal injury patients were all provided them to provide comfort.

I was in shock at having to make the decision, so I asked what a nerve-blocking medication was, and I was even more shocked by the response. The pain team described it as an old school antidepressant that would make Harrison comfortable. I asked what the side effects from such a medication were and they advised that they had no medical research to cover it. So, I tried again to find out more information by saying, 'Well, even if it's not scientific evidence, what is the anecdotal information relating to this kind of medication being used on a 13-year-old boy that up until this accident had full function and was healthy and happy, never having been on any medications or been diagnosed with anything?' They responded that they had no idea; so, I asked could they wait 24 hours for Joe, and I think about such a serious decision.

There are times in life when you must follow your gut, or what I like to fondly label my 'women's intuition'. I knew I was not a doctor, a chemist or a pharmacist, but I knew that if I were going to make a life-changing decision for my son that could result in him being a Christopher Reeve quadriplegic that was no longer a superman; I had to make sure I had left no stone unturned. So, in my usual enquiring and assertive manner, I asked to speak with the head of physiotherapy and the lead spinal department nurse that had been across Harrison's case. As fate would have it, they arrived in our room at the end of the day together.

I explained to both of them that since Harrison had been put into the screwless halo brace that he had the capability of agonising movement and had said he was starting to feel tingling in his hands and feet they were no longer numb.

They asked if I would agree to them trying to get Harrison out of bed to see if he was able to stand and what movement he may have. As they were mobilising him, they brought in another two physios to help move him and explained that for every movement Harrison would be in absolute agony and if they achieved getting him sitting on the side of the bed assisted that it would be exhausting for him. So much so that they would dose him with painkillers afterwards to sleep and recuperate.

That evening, they got him standing beside the bed; assisted by all of them. He was in so much pain he had tears rolling down his face continuously, he swore, and I had to move behind him so as he could not see me and instead have to work with the physio team without me at risk of asking for relief and for them to stop.

The Eye of the Storm

It was a monumental moment because even though he leant against his hospital bed weeping in pain and looking like a sack of flour, we all realised that he had the potential of full movement. The head of physio and lead spinal department nurse committed to go see the specialist spinal team straight away to explain what they had tried and discuss the potential. It was at that moment that I realised I needed to step up, educate myself and start to invest in understanding the medications he was being given, so that we could get the optimum result instead of a nerve-blocking medication.

Bright and early the next morning the team of spinal specialists arrived in Harrison's room to talk to us about the next steps. When we discussed what had happened the day prior with the pain management team and then Harrison standing and leaning against the side of the bed and him getting tingling feelings in his hands and feet, we worked out a plan.

I told them I wanted nothing to do with the 'pain in the arse team', the team formally known as the pain management team. The doctors joked that they are a team of anaesthetists that are used to dealing with patients that are asleep, so to encounter a lioness mother challenging them and asking questions would have been far out of their comfort zone. The doctors explained that Harrison is one of a kind because usually a C2 vertebra break occurs in motor vehicle accidents and kills adults. But because Harrison was yet to go through adolescence, he still a had a gap between his vertebrae and spinal column; so now that they knew that even though he had minimal feeling was in constant nerve pain and could stand; once the very badly broken vertebrae joined back together the nerves may regenerate. I then asked lots of questions about the existing medications Harrison was prescribed so I could understand their purpose, dosage rate and what each did. From that point, I started to oversee the schedule to ensure that each day I could report to the doctors and nurses about how long the medications were lasting, dose him before physio sessions so he could cope with the agony and rest afterwards.

The specialist team went away to work out what to do next; seeing they now understood the potential of this fit and healthy 13-year-old boy. For the first time, I had great hope that Harrison could obtain full mobility and lead a normal life. It was such relief for me to stop thinking about gripping onto whatever state of my former son I would leave hospital with and forecasting the disability care and complications he may experience in future. I knew extremely well what being a quadriplegic meant to a family because my grandfather was one.

The decision was made to operate on Harrison and install a screwed halo brace. The only female neurosurgeon took the lead on his surgery. The other male surgical team members explained that she turned to them before starting and said, 'I have a son about the same age as Harrison and he could fall off his bicycle any time and I would want to know that the best job was done on him so that every time he looks in the mirror, he doesn't have to see the scars as a reminder.' She commanded that operating theatre and had Harrison in traction on his stomach for three adjustments until she had the unbelievably bad C2 vertebra break aligned perfectly. Then instead of the screws being placed in his skull where they were visible; she spent more time and effort to place the front screws at the start of his hairline and the remainder around his head as per a usual application.

Harrison returned to the room amazingly comfortable and very sleepy. He slept for the longest duration since his accident. I must have dozed off to sleep, when around 2 am I heard the rustling of the bed covers and him making exertion noises – not a painful moan or scream that he had done previously. I leapt out of bed because I wondered what was going on. He started to talk fluently, 'I need to stand up, I need to stand up.' I was a bit panicked, since he had lain like a vegetable until this point, causing me to tell him I had to buzz the nurse to give me a hand to make sure it was okay to do so.

The Eye of the Storm

The same lead spinal nurse that had waited for Harrison's emergency flight arrival at the Brisbane Hospital, was also the same nurse that ensured she was rostered across his surgery and recovery and responded to Harrison's room and helped him get up. Harrison stayed awake all night and all the next day constantly moving. After seeing him lay still in the hospital bed for so long, I felt overwhelming joy at his agitation and attended to his every need. Sometimes, he would stop to have a lie down, but he could not rest because his legs and arms just wanted to keep on moving. I likened it to his body coming back online, the nerve ends leaping towards each other sending disjointed messages to move.

> *'Life can be a storm, but your hope is a rainbow and your friends and family are the gold.'*
> **Steve Maraboli**

CHAPTER 7

Batten Down the Hatches

'No storm can last forever. It will never rain 365 days consecutively. Keep in mind that trouble comes to pass, not to stay. Don't worry! No storm, not even the one in your life, can last forever.'
Iyanla Vanzant

We made the most of our hospital stay by participating in small routines, like going to the furthest wing to collect meals instead of the closest. This allowed me to remain grounded as I saw child cancer patients and complex child neuro patients that were also too young to look death in the face. Once I knew Harrison was comfortable, I would advise the nurse I was going for a walk late each afternoon. On the way back to the room, I would collect an apple juice, cheese and biscuits from the hospital's family visitor room for Joe and I to sit inside our top floor hospital room windows, watch the peak hour traffic congestion while we'd act like we were enjoying a relaxing sundowner and we'd phone the other three children to hear about their day.

In between medication, reading a novel to Harrison and physio appointments, we had visitors. The best visitors were the therapy dogs. I got the tingles the day Harrison said, 'I can feel the dog's hair.' The army visited him and a young man that had broken his C5 falling from a BMX bike in grade 12 and went to his graduation in a halo brace reached out to provide support and visited. Harrison also had high-profile visitors like the State Government Member and the City's Mayor show their support. These activities were reported in the newspaper and social media, so lots of people knew what had occurred and sent their well wishes for a speedy recovery, including the CEO from my work. I had not heard from my workplace in three months, and I saw his name come up on my mobile phone screen and I was in no mood to talk to him.

The CEO left a message saying that he had heard what had happened to our son and he hoped that he got well soon and that he wanted to talk to me so could I return his call.

This was another point of clarity. I had just spent weeks facing the worst-case scenario for a parent and was not stressed or anxious about it because we were in the best level of care, the medical staff listened to us and continuously provided a service to benefit us. Unlike my employer. I did not wish to speak with him. At this point, I could not have cared if I never heard or saw him again. He was incompetent at his job compared to the doctors treating Harrison. I asked Joe if he would speak to him and advise him that I would contact him when we returned home to arrange a face-to-face meeting. I do not like talking about serious matters over the phone because I am unable to read anyone's body language. Just as he had left me waiting at home for months, I was going to continue the focus on my family's wellbeing and his workplace issues could wait.

The media once again covered this serious time in our family's life.

THE OBSERVER

Tuesday, September 18, 2018

By Gregory Bray

'It's normally an injury that you die of in a car crash'

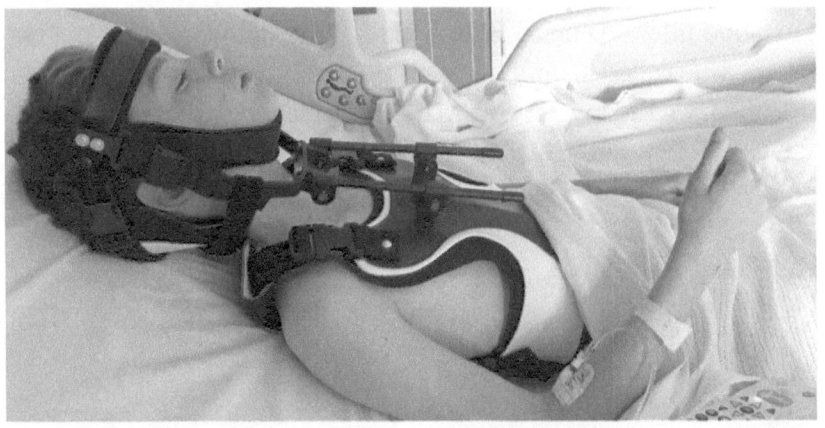

ROAD TO RECOVERY: Harrison McGuire is lucky to be alive after breaking his neck in a bicycle accident. Picture: Jen McGuire

A GOOD helmet, a mobile phone and the quick thinking of three boys saved 12-year-old Harrison McGuire's life two weeks ago.

Harrison's mother Jen McGuire said her son broke his neck after falling off his bicycle on September 4.

"Harry was with his twin brother Frazer and two friends riding on an abandoned construction site in Telina," she said.

"His bike ran into loose gravel and he fell off, landing directly on top of his head."

Harrison had a sustained an injury specialists in the orthopaedic spinal unit at The Lady Cilento Children's Hospital said they had never seen in a child before.

"He had clean broken the C2 bone in his neck," Mrs McGuire said.

"It's normally an adult injury that you die of in a car crash."

It was what happened next that saved her son's life.

"He was so brave, he knew he'd broken his neck and thought he was going to die," she said.

"As blood filled his neck, Frazer, Harrison's twin brother, rang his sisters, who called an ambulance while his two mates told him to lie still and used their water bottles to rinse off the blood from his cuts."

Harrison McGuire at this year's HookUp fishing competition
Picture: Jen McGuire

Harrison was taken to Gladstone Hospital.

"The doctors at the Gladstone Hospital were great, but they didn't have the specialists and drugs needed to treat this sort of injury.

"When the specialists in Brisbane saw the gravity of the injury they immediately sent up a specialised retrieval team on a Royal Flying Doctors plane."

Within hours Harrison was at The Lady Cilento Children's Hospital where a team of orthopaedic surgeons were standing by.

"They did an MRI and immediately ordered a Halo Brace to stabilise him," Mrs McGuire said.

"There's only one in Australia."

Harrison's entire body had pins and needles and there was a very real danger he could choke on his own spit.

"Once they told him he wasn't going to die and how much movement he had and they told him he would walk again, he was relieved," she said.

"We've got a long way to go though."

THE OBSERVER

Tuesday, September 18, 2018

By Gregory Bray

'Special moment': Dog aids boy's recovery after crash

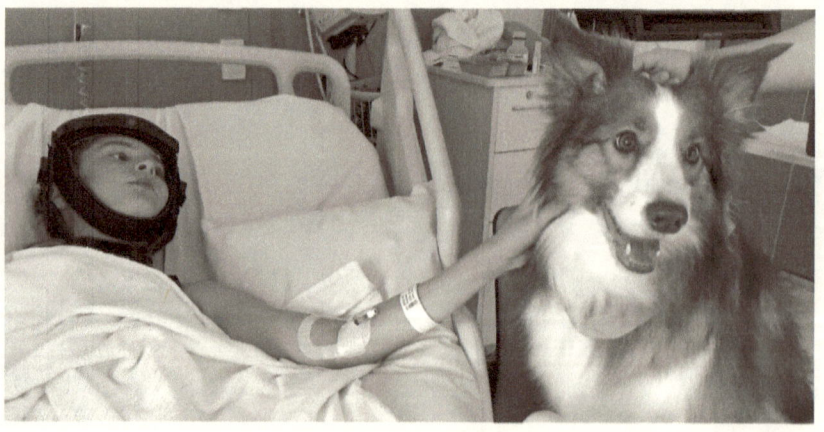

ANIMAL THERAPY: Harrison McGuire with Ginger a therapy dog at the Lady Cilento Children's Hospital Brisbane Picture: Jen McGuire

THREE days after breaking his neck Harrison McGuire was lying heavily sedated in a hospital bed in The Lady Cilento Hospital in Brisbane.

His mother Jenny McGuire admitted his recovery didn't seem to be going anywhere at this stage.

On September 4 the 12-year-old broke his neck after falling from his bicycle.

"He hadn't improved, he was in too much pain," she said.

"All the body's nerves go through that part of the spine.

"He had pins and needles all over, but all his muscles were spasming, he was contorting and shrinking up.

"His entire body was going into overload, if a butterfly had landed on his skin he would have screamed."

The doctors prescribed pain killers and muscle relaxants.

"During that time they had sandbags and tape keeping his head stable.

That morning Mrs McGuire was asked if her son wanted some animal therapy.

"He was drugged to the eyeballs to keep him sleeping," she said.

"I said no, because Harrison wasn't in a good way, and I thought they'd put some fluffy little yapper on the bed that he wouldn't really be interested in anyway because we've got two red border collies at home.

"But when I saw this magnificently groomed border collie wander past I immediately changed my mind.

The dog, Ginger, hopped up on a chair next to Harrison's bed and Mrs McGuire woke him up and placed his hand on her fur.

"It was such a special moment," she said.

"The best part was he smiled and in spite of the pins and needles he said he could feel Ginger's fur and it felt like his dog Iggy.

"It was amazing."

CORPORATE STORM

THE OBSERVER

Tuesday, September 18, 2018

By Gregory Bray

Fuel mix up helps mum cope with son's near-death injury

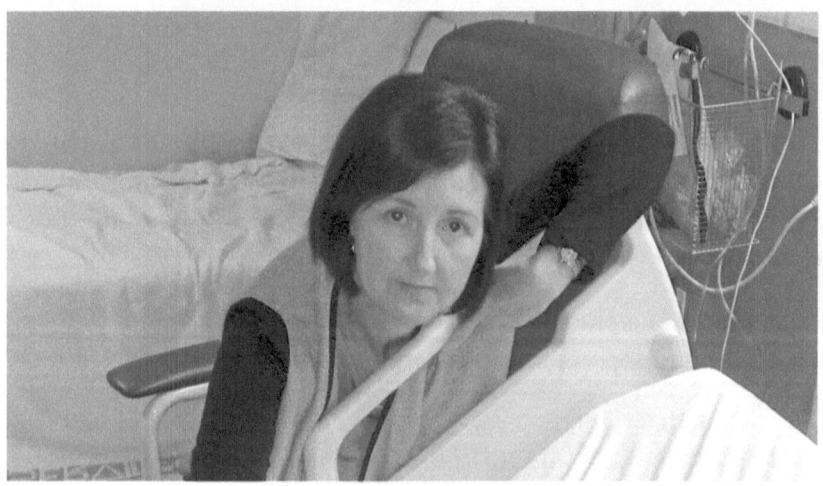

LUCKY TO BE ALIVE: Jen McGuire with her son Harrison at The Lady Cilento Children's Hospital Picture: Jen McGuire

THE day 12-year-old Harrison McGuire broke his neck, Mrs McGuire's husband Joe flew down to Brisbane with him.

"To be able to care for someone who is near death, you need to be brave so they're brave," she said.

Instead, Mrs McGuire packed her bags, organised the house and family and hopped in the car at first light the next day.

"I filled the LandCruiser with what I thought was diesel," she said.

"In fact I had two-thirds filled it with unleaded."

Mrs McGuire said the fuel mix-up was a blessing in disguise.

"It literally stopped me in more ways than one," she said.

"I was running on adrenaline and now I had to slow down and wait.

"The RACQ gave me the choice to be taken back to Gladstone and get the fuel drained, or I could continue on to the Lady Cilento car park."

"I asked to be taken back to Gladstone.

"Dealing with my son and a broken-down car in the city would have been too much."

"Unbelievably, I was brought back by a tow-truck driver who was an ex-ambulance officer and he was able to explain everything."

While the car was being fixed, the specialist visited Harrison and confirmed he would recover.

"Once I knew Harrison was safe I got a good night's sleep and set off the next day.

"The universe was really looking out for us."

CORPORATE STORM

THE OBSERVER

Wednesday, September 19, 2018

By Gregory Bray

'Tears of joy': Mum recounts son's first steps after crash

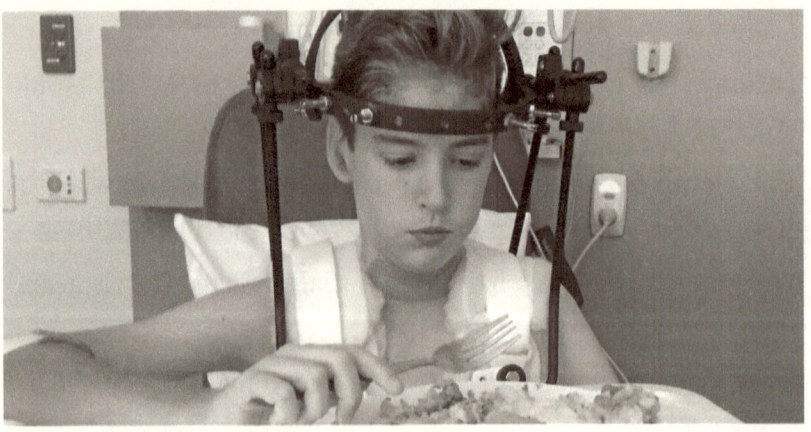

UP AND EAT'EM: Harrison McGuire is recovering in the Lady Cilento Children's Hospital. Picture: Jen McGuire

FOUR days after breaking his neck in a bicycle accident Harrison McGuire took his first wobbly steps on the long road to recovery.

His mother, Jenni, said it was an amazing moment.

"His father, Joe, was back in Gladstone playing a grand final hockey game," she said.

"But Harrison was in the grand final of his life."

With assistance he was able to shuffle to the window of his hospital room.

"He was so brave," Mrs McGuire said.

"The pain was so bad that tears were running down his face.

"Tears were running down mine too but they were tears of joy."

Harrison McGuire recovery: Harrison McGuire is walking again after breaking his neck in a bicycle accident

With the aid of the halo brace, specialists and painkillers, Harrison is learning to adjust to life in recovery.

"He's exhausted from the pain, he's so hypersensitive," she said.

"All his nerves are inflamed so his body spasms and contorts and his skin feels like it's been badly burned, it's very painful.

"The more sleep, the more he heals."

They expect to be in Brisbane for the rest of this week.

"We're hoping he'll be able to come back to Gladstone this weekend," Mrs McGuire said.

"It's still early days and he's got lots of rehab ahead of him."

There was one special sign Harrison was on the mend.

"He laughed for the first time after watching a silly video of Boots the Cat," Mrs McGuire said.

"No sooner had he laughed then he had a poo at last.

"Laughter really is the best medicine."

THE OBSERVER

Wednesday, September 19, 2018

By Gregory Bray

Gladstone gets behind Harrison's recovery

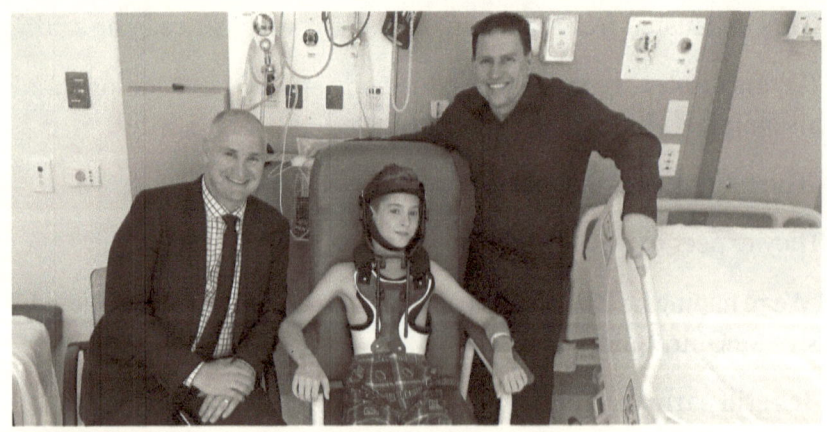

HIGH PROFILE VISITORS: Harrison McGuire was surprised by a visit from State Member Glenn Butcher and Mayor Matt Burnett Picture: Jen McGuire

ON DAYS when Harrison McGuire is feeling low, his parents boost his spirits by showing him all the support he's getting from people in Gladstone.

Mum Jenni said the family had received hundreds of calls and messages.

"The staff at the Lady Cilento (Children's Hospital) have been amazed at how much support Harrison's been getting," she said.

"It says a lot about Gladstone."

Mrs McGuire is currently sleeping at the hospital with her son, while her husband, Joe, is staying with Grant and Leith Mitchell, Gladstone friends now living in Brisbane.

But the family was surprised when two special visitors dropped in to visit Harrison.

"Mayor Matt Burnett and State Member for Gladstone Glenn Butcher were in Brisbane for a meeting and popped in afterwards," Mrs McGuire said.

"We were so grateful for their visit.

"Matt said Harrison's rehab chair looks like the mayor's chair and that's what the staff are calling it now."

Harrison is slowly recovering and continues to have nightmares about the accident.

"He has a massive amount of rehab in front of him but a huge village supporting him," Mrs McGuire said.

THE OBSERVER

Friday, September 21, 2018

By Gregory Bray

Crash victim Harrison is keen to get back home to Gladstone

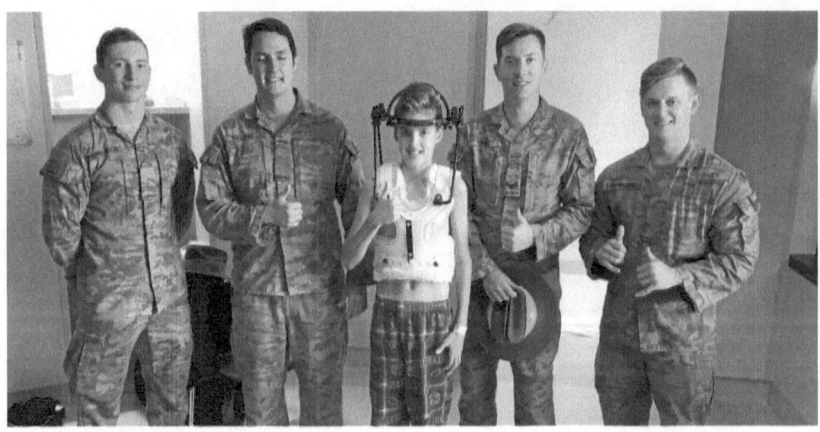

LITTLE TROOPER: Harrison McGuire with a group of soldiers who were visiting patients in The Lady Cilento Children's Hospital. Picture: Jen McGuire

NEARLY three weeks after breaking his neck in a bicycle accident, Harrison McGuire is making an excellent recovery.

His mother Jenni McGuire said the break was one of the worst the specialists at The Lady Cilento Children's Hospital have ever seen.

"He had a 5mm gap in the bone," she said.

"That's why they were so surprised Harrison doesn't have paralysis or brain damage.

"On Monday afternoon they put him in traction and sedated him and re-aligned the break which closed the gap.'

On Tuesday morning Harrison woke up after surgery and announced the pins and needles which had covered his entire body had gone.

"He walked around the room," Mrs McGuire said.

"Afterwards the orthopaedic surgeons tightened up all the pins they put into his skull to make sure they remain in place.

"He's still in a lot of pain, but we can manage this."

Harrison's recovery has been so impressive the family have been told he will be back home much sooner than expected.

Mrs McGuire and her husband Joe have been given some training to assist Harrison for the next six weeks.

"Joe and I have been shown how to sterilise and take care of the screws penetrating his skin and skull,

"They'll be teleconferencing with the Gladstone Hospital to make sure we're doing the right thing.

"And all going to plan in six weeks time we'll be back in Brisbane to have the brace taken off and he'll start the spinal specialists physio."

She said at that point the specialist will be looking for any deficiencies.

"They told us that that it will be things like turning his head and vibrations," Mrs McGuire said.

"We'll have months of rehabilitation until hopefully we get our son back."

Harry's break is aligned & healing. He's no longer got pins & needles and his arms & legs are really restless, so we keep on hearing "I want to get up!" So his body is coming back online. He's in alot of pain but this is being managed. We forecast he'll be home soon. Therefore, I'm going to return home earlier to get the house organised with mobility equipment and his favourite mushy foods. Joe McGuire & Harry will fly home once he's up to it.

Batten Down the Hatches

When we returned home from hospital a couple of weeks later, I attended an appointment with the CEO. At this meeting, the CEO, of course, used the icebreaker of wishing to understand what had happened with Harrison's accident and treatment. Then he asked me if I was feeling well enough to meet. He then went on to advise me that the serious allegations that had been raised against me were completely unfounded and there would be no investigation. He then said I was right to return to work as soon as possible and every day that I stayed away from that point would be taken as personal leave. I responded by letting him know that we were settling into Harrison's home care routine and based on Joe's shift work I would return to work part days of the week and that I would send him an email with the planned days of work. I asked him if any workplace performance management or training had been undertaken with the union representatives that had inappropriately treated the trainees and he responded with nothing. All these people were still in the same workplace without being held responsible and accountable to make any improvements. I advised that I would not be comfortable returning to my old job, and he asked for me to send him an email containing my suggestions of where I could work in the organisation.

After a week of email communications between the CEO and myself, we had agreed on the flexible workplace arrangements of me taking personal leave on the days that Joe worked so as I could care for Harrison and me designing, creating, delivering and training the improvements I had previously identified to the new Procure to Pay System and commencing a Contractor Management System.

****

The first day I arrived at work after five months of being away I met my newly appointed general manager. He advised me that I could go to my old office and collect my work materials with an escort. I was not provided badge swipe access to all the buildings, facilities or access to the businesses' computer network. A copy of a confidential letter between the CEO and myself containing some information concerning the ongoing Crime and Corruption Commission investigation was in his possession. For an employee that had stood up for the inappropriate treatment of two young female trainees and was offered hush money to walk away and threatened with serious allegations against me that were now unfounded, I was not being given the red-carpet treatment. I sucked it up. Kept my mouth shut because I was pleased to be walking back into the workplace after such a long time. I held my head up, kept my mouth shut as I did not wish to project any past negativity onto my new relationship as my new general manager showed me to my office.

After a couple of days, I was called to a meeting with the CEO where he once again asked me if I was feeling well enough to be at work. I raised my concerns that I was to be provided an escort to my old office to obtain materials, I did not have access across the entire business like a used to, I had no computer access to the levels I did in the past, and I was concerned that the confidential letter between him and I relating to the CCC investigation was in my new general manager's possession. He responded that everyone knew about the confidential CCC investigation; because the interviews had been planned right here in the workplace, so people saw people coming and going so were talking about it. I found this hard to believe so I left his office and met with the Board's company secretary to ask the same.

The company secretary advised that all the CCC investigation meetings were held in an independent off-site location, just as mine had been. Shortly after me raising this, the new Chairman of the Board sent a letter to each of the CCC investigation's subjects, witnesses and a copy of the correspondence to myself to remind all of them of the confidentiality requirements of the investigation. Even though the CEO was still trying to intimidate me, I knew the Board were taking the investigation seriously and trying to maintain the integrity of the process.

Batten Down the Hatches

I refer to a new Chairman of the Board; because while I was off work and in Brisbane with Harrison, the old Chairman of the Board (who had been the only person to help me by doing the legally compliant action of advising the CCC of my complaint) did not have his chairmanship contract renewed.

****

Over the next six months, I delivered the commercial project work within the time frame I had forecast and trained around 150 people in the application of a contractor management system and the improvements to the Procure to Pay System to comply with Government legislation. It was therapeutic for me to stand in front of these fellow employees and educate them on ethical procurement, probity processes, separation of duties, open market approaches, prequalification of contractors, risk management of contracts, strategic sourcing and the extensive list continued. Whatever the rumours were that had been spread about me, I held my head high, kept my mouth shut and educated people on the legal requirements.

The downside to these six months was that I was not invited to team meetings, department meetings, leadership meetings, any training or workshop type of forums, a Christmas Party and one morning the CEO hosted a Christmas morning tea for all the corporate staff in my building and I was not invited. He made it noticeably clear that he had not welcomed me back to work and he was going to continue to make my life difficult.

****

Three months into my return to work, I was invited to a meeting hosted by the Chairman of the Board, company secretary with a human resources consultant in attendance. At this meeting, I was handed a letter by the Chairman to advise that it was a favourable outcome of the CCC investigation. Every serious allegation I had raised had been substantiated and the CEO remained stood down from attending the workplace. He thanked me for my courage in raising these matters and introduced the HR consultant as the new independent person to the workplace that would place a fresh set of eyes across any serious HR matters and anything concerning myself, seeing the still employed HR general manager was a subject of the CCC investigation and the mismanagement of my claims that the HR general manager would not handle anything related to myself in future. The company secretary told me not to crack open the champagne too early, but rather to go home from work now, read it in detail and quietly celebrate while maintaining confidentiality of the investigation.

Private and Confidential

By hand delivery

Dear Jennifer,

Finalisation of Confidential Investigation

I refer to:

- (a) Your complaint to the Corporation;
- (b) The Corporation's correspondence;
- (c) The meeting today with the company secretary, where you were handed a copy of this letter.

Background

The Corporation takes employee complaints very seriously and, as you know, the Corporation's Board initiated an investigation into your complaints with the assistance of an external investigator (**Investigation**).

Batten Down the Hatches

The investigation is now complete. The Corporation has considered and continues to work through what actions are necessary in light of the investigation findings.

The purpose of this letter is to provide you with details regarding the finalisation of the Investigation.

It is important that you understand the Investigation including any findings, outcomes and/or recommendations are private, confidential and privileged. However, the Corporation is able to provide you with the following update in relation to the allegations and findings as they pertain to you.

Outcome of Investigation

With respect to the complaints raised by you, the Investigation substantiated that:

1. *There was an unreasonable and unjustifiable delay in attending to… bullying and harassment complaints…the investigation identified that this breached the:*
    a. *Corporation Equity, Diversity, Harassment and Discrimination Standard because the reported breaches were not managed as soon as practicable after the breaches were reported; and*
    b. *Corporation Managing Discipline Specification as there was no prompt attempt to resolve the unacceptable behaviour.*
2. *The Corporation acted unreasonably and/or not in accordance with relevant policies and procedures when it requested investigations into complaints against you.*

Specifically, the investigation identified that the following breaches of the Corporation's Managing Discipline Specification and Code of Conduct occurred:

Managing Discipline Specification

   a. *The process was not conducted in an open and transparent manner;*
   b. *You were not afforded due process and natural justice;*
   c. *You were not provided with information on the matter under discussion;*
   d. *You were not provided with an opportunity to state your case and not treated fair and equitably;*

Code of Conduct

   e. *Decisions made with regard to you were not made objectively and with proper regard to rights and obligations;*
   f. *You were not treated with adequate respect;*
   g. *A conflict of interest existed which adversely affected the manner and decision making in which the investigation regarding you occurred; and*
   h. *Certain decisions of Corporation employees were tainted by favouritism, self-interest and/or bias.*

3. *Corporation acted unreasonably and/or not in accordance with relevant policies and procedures when it requested investigations into additional complaints made against you.*

Batten Down the Hatches

Specifically, the investigation identified that the following breaches of Corporation policies and codes of conduct occurred:

Managing Discipline Specification

   a. *You were not afforded due process and natural justice;*
   b. *The investigation was not conducted in a fair and objective manner; and*
   c. *The specification's requirements for standing aside an employee was not met;*

Code of Conduct

   d. *You were not treated with respect and decisions regarding you were not made objectively and with proper regard to rights and obligations; and*

   e. *Decisions regarding you were not made free from favouritism, self-interest and bias.*

4. *Corporation offered you a mutual separation package to leave your employment...*

   Specifically, the investigator noted that:

   a. *You rejected the offer...the same day you were stood aside pending an investigation into complaints made against you; and*
   b. *Corporation used the investigation in an inappropriate manner to 'encourage' you to accept mutual separation.*

The offer of mutual separation package was made prior to commencement of the investigation. In doing so, contrary to the Corporation Managing Discipline Specification and Corporation Code of Conduct, the Corporation did not:

> *a. Identify and or promptly attempt to resolve any instance of unacceptable employee behaviour and/or unresolved performance concerns;*
> *b. Afford Ms McGuire due process and natural justice.*

The Corporation considers that such conduct is inconsistent with Corporation policies and procedures and the behaviour it expects from all of its employees.

Next Steps

As result of the investigation, the Corporation will now move to close the Investigation and work with relevant employees on the need for:

> *a. Policy reviews; and*
> *b. Training*

The Corporation are keen to ensure that, moving forward, all employees know and understand:

> *a. Corporation policies and procedures;*
> *b. What is acceptable conduct in the workplace; and*
> *c. What is unacceptable conduct in the workplace.*

Batten Down the Hatches

This may include training, coaching and/or disciplinary action for any and all employees directly involved in any substantiated allegations and more broadly for the organisation. What action the Corporation decides to take in relation to any required disciplinary action is a private and confidential matter between the Corporation and each employee.

For clarity, please note that as a result of this Investigation and the matters that were investigated, we can confirm that your conduct is not subject to any disciplinary action.

Your current role – we appreciate your ongoing work.

The Corporation again wishes to thank you for taking the time and effort in bringing these concerns to our attention. The Corporation appreciates your involvement in this Investigation as it has enabled the Corporation to understand the Complaint and determine what actions needed to be taken as a result of the Investigation.

Yours sincerely...

The Chairman then asked me if I had lodged my matter with any other organisation or lawyer, to which I responded that I had not, other than seeking legal advice in the very beginning when I thought I was being offered hush money. He said he had no idea what this second envelope was about; so, I asked him if he wanted me to open it up in this meeting and let him know.

The envelope contained a letter requesting me as a witness to a Treasury investigation into the workplace's Executive, starting with the previous Chairman of the Board. I had no idea what this was going to be about and here is where I started to feel overwhelmed.

I showed the letter to the Chairman and company secretary and asked if the Board would support me in contributing to this investigation. To which they responded favourably and said that the new HR consultant would be my support person and if I needed anything to contact him in future. The Chairman reminded me of how thankful the Board were that I had raised the original issues and said they would support me in the Treasury investigation. I asked if I could digest this news and get back to the company secretary with my arrangements.

I went home from work straight away that afternoon and still was not game enough to talk to anyone about anything in person or over the phone. Joe and I sat on the back veranda and read the four-page letter containing the successful CCC investigation outcomes repeatedly. We shared a bottle of champagne and rejoiced at our success. Joe had been more than a supportive, understanding husband – he believed in me and what I had stood up for and had been with me every step of the way. We were proud of what we had done; but could not shout it from the mountain tops and instead once again cherished the moment together.

After an excellent night's sleep, the next morning I understood what the next part of this process was about. It became clear to me that the CCC investigation scope covered the girl's inappropriate treatment and the mismanagement of me. The CCC investigation did not cover the Executive and the legal non-compliance I had detected and raised with the CEO. I would later find out that this was true. A CCC investigation only covered lower-level employees. When a Government Owned Corporation's Executive is accused of misconduct, the relevant department (in this case, the Treasury) must investigate.

The media covered this progress.

THE OBSERVER

Friday, October 5, 2018

By: Tegan Annett

What's next for complaint about GPC

THE Crime and Corruption Commission has referred a complaint about Gladstone Ports Corporation to the Queensland Treasury for investigation.

The complaint, received and assessed by the commission, was referred to the state authority this week.

While the details of the complaint are unknown, it's believed to be related to how the business is run.

A commission spokesperson said after assessing the complaint they determined it needed to be referred to the Queensland Treasury.

"It will be subject to the commission's monitoring," they said.

"It is important to note all allegations should be treated as unsubstantiated until a final outcome is reached."

The commission often refers complaints to other departments, agencies or the Queensland Police Service.

When an agency is directed by the commission to investigate a complaint it must provide regular reports and finalise the matter within a specified time period.

A Queensland Treasury spokesman said: "In compliance with this notice, Treasury will undertake an investigation and report to the CCC, which will closely monitor progress of this matter."

On August 17 the complaint "raising concerns about administration" at the GPC was referred by the State Government to the commission.

A joint statement from Treasurer Jackie Trad and Transport Minister Mark Bailey at the time said the information was recently brought to the attention of GPC shareholding ministers, who reported it to the Queensland Treasury.

Batten Down the Hatches

The following morning, I arrived in the company secretary's office to respond favourably to the Treasury letter. I asked that she request Treasury to use my personal email and mobile number as had the CCC, as no information was contained on the workplace computer network. I asked that anytime I needed to leave the workplace to meet or attend to anything related to this Treasury investigation, I would not be required to apply for leave or notify anyone because I did not trust anyone in the Executive to remain confidential. I asked to be able to leave the workplace for whatever the time required without any explanation to anyone if it related to me responding to the Treasury investigation. The last request I made was for the Treasury Department to access the CCC investigation because I did not want to have to go over old ground. I felt that I had put my life on hold, sustained an attack from the Executive that should have done the right thing and not attacked me. All the Executive had done up to this point in time was to try to intimidate me to cause me to run away. I realised that I was now completely out of my comfort zone and heading into the unknown. I had started this process for a good reason, and I was going to get the courage to continue to see it through until the finish. It took a lot for me to refocus my energy because I felt like I had won the battle, but I suddenly realised that this was turning into a war that, from my low level in the organisation, I was unaware of the military game plan. Still to this day I do not know what Executives turned on who and what dirt they had on each other, but one by one I was called on to be interviewed as a witness to the Treasury investigation.

****

In March 2018, I received a letter requesting my participation in an interview. The letter advised that I was being called as a witness to the Treasury investigation and the subject was the former Chairman of the Board. This perplexed me because I had very little interaction with him, so I had no idea what it was concerning. However, no sooner than I received the letter than I had an anonymous community complaint phone into the

Corporation's reception advising the work vehicle I normally drove had been seen speeding at 90 kilometres per hour through a 40 kilometres per hour school zone that morning. The complainant identified the registration of the vehicle and a description of the driver that matched me. The female voice did not wish to be identified, did not leave their contact details to verify. Very fortunately, I had been in meetings all morning, so people could vouch for me. However, interestingly enough, within hours of the complaint being communicated across the Corporation's weekly events management report to the business I was in a room with my new general manager and a human resources team member to be advised it was the Corporation's standard process to conduct an investigation into community complaints against employees. It was amazing how the Executive could act so quickly to investigate me, yet they could not investigate the illegal activity by union reps against young, female trainees.

I attended the Treasury investigation interview and answered all their questions. However, I had no information to provide them that was of any concern. The former Chairman was the only person that did the right, legal action by me and the female trainees. Up until he notified the Board and CCC of my and the trainee's treatment, the Executive were intimidating and trying to get rid of me. I was relieved many months later to hear in the media that he was cleared.

Newspapers reported on the Chairman being cleared.

THE OBSERVER

Tuesday, September 1, 2020

By Rodney Stevens

Crime watchdog clears former Gladstone Ports Corp chairman

THE CRIME and Corruption Commission has elected to take no action against former Gladstone Ports Corporation Chairman and CEO Leo Zussino following an investigation by Queensland Treasury.

On August 17, 2018, a complaint made to the CCC against Mr Zussino "raising concerns about administration" was referred to the Queensland State Government.

A joint statement from Treasurer Jackie Trad and Transport Minister Mark Bailey at the time said the information was recently brought to the attention of GPC shareholding ministers, who reported it to the Queensland Treasury.

It is standard practice for the CCC to refer complaints to government agencies, including Queensland police, for investigation.

Finer details of the complaint remain unknown.

When questioned by *The Observer* in 2018, a CCC spokesman said after assessing the complaint they determined it needed to be referred to the Queensland Treasury.

"It will be subject to the commission's monitoring," they said.

"It is important to note all allegations should be treated as unsubstantiated until a final outcome is reached."

At the time, a treasury spokesman said "In compliance with this notice, Treasury will undertake an investigation and report to the CCC, which will closely monitor progress of this matter."

Today Mr Zussino emailed *The Observer* a media statement, which was BCC'd (blind carbon copied) to his legal adviser Nicholas Patrick.

"An investigation by Queensland Treasury, monitored by the Crime and Corruption Commission, has concluded with no action taken against Mr Leo Zussino," the statement said.

"Mr. Zussino would like to thank his family and friends for their support throughout this period.

"Mr. Zussino served as Chairman of the Gladstone Ports Corporation from 1990 to 1999, before being appointed Chief Executive Officer in 2000 a position he held until 2013, Mr Zussino was reappointed as Chairman in 2015 for a further 3-year term."

In 2013, Mr Zussino stood down as GPC chairman at the request of the then LNP Government, after Gladstone Harbour was labelled a "toxic wasteland."

At the time Mr Zussino blamed activists for their scaremongering rhetoric surrounding the impacts of the dredging of the harbour.

He said the then campaign against dredging Gladstone Harbour was a classic example of how easy it was to spread misinformation.

"[The activist movement] knows that there is not a man, woman or child in this nation who wants harm to come to the Great Barrier Reef and it ruthlessly exploits that fact," Mr Zussino told *The Financial Review*.

"If Australia is to continue on the path of sustainable development, industry leaders and politicians alike need to articulate the sustainable development agenda with the same rigour and persistence as the green movement promotes its agenda."

Activists claimed the Gladstone Harbour seafood industry had been destroyed, which investigations attributed to the 2011 floods.

Seagrasses which were killed following the floods began to flourish, resulting in a bumper seafood crop in 2013, reported The Financial Review.

The media statement noted Mr Zussino's achievements as GPC chairman included initiating and implementing the GPC 50 years' strategic plan, growth of trade from 30 mtpa to more than 120 mtpa during his tenure, an increase in wharves from 10 to 20, and the creation of more than 450 permanent jobs.

THE OBSERVER

Tuesday, September 1, 2020

By Rodney Stevens

Watchdog says Ports Corp inquiry 'appropriate'

A QUEENSLAND Treasury investigation which cleared former Gladstone Ports Corporation chairman and CEO Leo Zussino of corrupt conduct claims has been given the green light by the Crime and Corruption Commission.

Today Mr Zussino issued a media statement saying "An investigation by Queensland Treasury, monitored by the Crime and Corruption Commission, has concluded with no action taken against Mr Leo Zussino."

This was reported in the story Crime Watchdog clears former Gladstone Ports Corp chairman.

The Gladstone Observer put a number of questions to the Crime and Corruption Commission CCC and Queensland Treasury.

The Observer was then called by Queensland Treasury Media spokesman with questions about Mr Zussino's statement.

The spokesman said he wanted to ensure Queensland Treasury and the CCC were "on the same page" about the issue.

Following that conversation, the CCC issued the following media statement to *The Observer*.

"The Crime and Corruption Commission (CCC) referred allegations of corrupt conduct relating to the former Gladstone Ports Corporation Chairman and CEO to Queensland Treasury to investigate," a CCC spokesman said.

"The CCC determined it would monitor Queensland Treasury's investigation.

"The CCC has reviewed the investigation conducted by Queensland Treasury and has determined it was conducted appropriately."

The CCC would not elaborate on questions posed by The Observer about the allegations, who made them, what the allegations related to, or who the allegations involved.

"It is not appropriate for the CCC to comment on the specifics of the allegations or the investigation conducted by Queensland Treasury," the CCC spokesman said.

"The CCC does not confirm or deny any potential complaint or investigation unless a party directly related to a matter makes it publicly known first.

"On that basis, the CCC declines to comment further."

The GPC has been contacted for comment and told The Observer this afternoon it was working on a statement.

THE OBSERVER

Wednesday, September 2, 2020

By Rodney Stevens

What Ports Corp said about CCC inquiry

THE Gladstone Ports Corporation has stayed silent on the Crime and Corruption Commission and Queensland Treasury investigation involving former CEO and chairman Leo Zussino.

Mr Zussino issued a statement at 12.09am on Tuesday, stating the investigation had concluded.

"An investigation by Queensland Treasury, monitored by the Crime and Corruption Commission, has concluded with no action taken against Mr Leo Zussino," the statement said.

The CCC responded to questions from *The Observer* with the following statement.

"The Crime and Corruption Commission referred allegations of corrupt conduct relating to the former Gladstone Ports Corporation Chairman and CEO to Queensland Treasury to investigate.

"The CCC determined it would monitor Queensland Treasury's investigation.

"The CCC has reviewed the investigation conducted by Queensland Treasury and has determined it was conducted appropriately.

"It is not appropriate for the CCC to comment on the specifics of the allegations or the investigation conducted by Queensland Treasury.

"The CCC does not confirm or deny any potential complaint or investigation unless a party directly related to a matter makes it publicly known first.

"On that basis, the CCC declines to comment further."

The Observer contacted the GPC with a number of questions following the release of Mr Zussino's statement.

The questions included, who reported the alleged conduct, when was the conduct alleged to have occurred, who did the alleged conduct involve and what were the details of the alleged conduct.

The GPC replied to the questions with a brief statement.

"It would not be appropriate for GPC to comment on the specifics of the allegations or the investigation undertaken by Queensland Treasury," a spokesperson said.

"We must respect the requirement for confidentiality in relation to such matters."

CORPORATE STORM

In May 2018, the Board terminated the CEO's position with the Corporation because of the CCC investigation findings, which was subsequently reported on by the media.

THE OBSERVER

Tuesday, May 21, 2019

By Sarah Vogler

Ports boss sacked after complaint

GLADSTONE Ports chief executive Peter O'Sullivan has been sacked by the board following an investigation into his handling of a "staff disciplinary matter".

It also comes a week after the port was thrust into national headlines when The Courier-Mail revealed a contractor working at the port was suspended after questioning Bill Shorten at a barbecue during the federal election campaign.

"Following a thorough and extensive investigation of concerns raised last year about the conduct of Gladstone Ports Corporation's chief executive officer, the board has made the decision to terminate Mr Peter O'Sullivan's tenure as CEO and will immediately start a merit-based search for GPC's new leader," the board said in a statement last night.

"Mr O'Sullivan was suspended on December 13 last year, on full pay, and has had no involvement with the day-to-day operations of the port since that time.

"The substantiated complaint related to Mr O'Sullivan's role in a staff disciplinary matter."

Staff were last night notified of the board's decision via an internal memo, with acting chief executive Craig Walker to continue acting in the role.

Deputy Premier Jackie Trad has asked Treasury to investigate.

"In undertaking any investigation, it would be important to ascertain whether any direction, formal or informal, was given after the Federal Leader of the Opposition Mr Shorten was embarrassed by the question from the contractor," Ms Frecklington said.

THE OBSERVER

Tuesday, May 21, 2019

By Tegan Annett and Mark Zita

'Grave concerns': Former ports CEO speaks out over sacking

Play Video
EXCLUSIVE: Peter O'Sullivan Speaks Out

EXCLUSIVE: Peter O'Sullivan is preparing a legal challenge against his former employer Gladstone Ports Corporation after he was accused of misconduct and sacked as chief executive officer.

The former Ports boss of three years was suspended with pay in December last year while an investigation was conducted into a complaint about how he handled a staff disciplinary matter.

On Monday night, GPC confirmed Mr O'Sullivan had been dismissed after a "thorough and extensive" investigation.

Mr O'Sullivan refutes the allegations and claims the corporation's board was trying to "push him out".

Speaking exclusively to *The Observer* he said the past five months had been "extremely difficult" for him, his wife and two children.

"It's been extremely distressing for the entire family," he said.

"I was the principal of the high school before this and I pride myself that I've always held myself on high ethical standards.

"You don't sleep, it's very difficult to maintain your friendship circles too.

"You go out and people ask 'what's going on' and you can't talk about it."

In December 2018, Mr O'Sullivan was made aware of 12 allegations made towards him.

He said after he replied to the allegations 10 were dropped, with the two remaining relating to an investigation which he ordered into a workplace complaint.

He said the board alleged he had ordered the investigation for an "improper purpose" and he was "vague and inconsistent" during the investigation.

Issues with the board's investigation and decision have been referred to the Crime and Corruption Commission by Mr O'Sullivan.

He has also sought legal advice on how to challenge the allegations.

"It's extremely disappointing for myself and my family for (the board) to do this and to have your name splashed on the front page of the paper when you firmly believe that you haven't done anything that relates to misconduct that requires a dismissal," he said.

Mr O'Sullivan claims some members of the board should not have been involved in the decision-making process, because they were among those who made the allegations.

"I've never been part of an organisation which would allow someone who's made an allegation to be part of the procedural process," he said.

"I'm not someone to stand idly by when an unfair and unreasonable process is being done.

"It gives me grave concerns in how GPC is being managed."

Mr O'Sullivan said his concerns about the board of the Queensland Government-owned corporation began in August last year.

"To see the port on the front page of the *Courier Mail* and *The Australian* for all the wrong reasons, it's extremely disappointing and the shareholding ministers need to step in and take some action," he said.

"What's disappointing for me is it destroys the reputation of the port."

In August last year, former chairman Leo Zussino was stood aside.

At the time a complaint had been made to the Crime and Corruption Commission regarding the way the business was run.

The complaint was referred to Queensland Treasury in October last year and today the department told *The Observer* its investigation was ongoing.

Queensland Ports Minister Mark Bailey said the government made it clear GPC's focus should be "squarely on growing trade, supporting local jobs and our regional economy".

He said Mr O'Sullivan's dismissal was the result of a thorough investigation.

Chairman Peter Corones said in a statement to *The Observer* last night the board's decision was a result of its own investigation.

Mr Corones defended the port's senior management team and said it would be "business as usual" for customers, stakeholders and the community until a new CEO was appointed.

He did not respond to questions about if the allegations were part of a bid by the board to "push out" Mr O'Sullivan.

He said GPC would immediately start a merit-based search for its new leader.

Craig Walker, who has been acting chief executive officer since late last year, will continue in the role until a permanent replacement is found.

The Observer

Tuesday, May 21, 2019

By Mark Zita

Ports Corp tight-lipped on CEO saga

UPDATE 1:20PM: GLADSTONE Ports Corporation has refused to comment about the dismissal of chief executive officer Peter O'Sullivan.

Earlier today, The Observer asked the corporation questions in relation to the circumstances surrounding the move and if the Queensland Government had a say in the matter.

GPC did not respond to any questions and said it would not comment further on the matter.

The company published a brief statement on its website about Mr O'Sullivan's dismissal this morning.

UPDATE 11.00AM: THE search is on for Peter O'Sullivan's replacement after the Gladstone Ports Corporation board dismissed the chief executive officer over questions about his conduct.

The now-former CEO was suspended on full pay on December 13.

The Courier-Mail said last night workers were told via an internal memo that Mr O'Sullivan had since been dismissed.

Mr O'Sullivan was appointed as CEO in July 2016.

His duties included directing and controlling business activities, leading GPC in meeting short and long-term objectives and being responsible for the management and organisational structure of the corporation.

Mr O'Sullivan spoke openly about the potential opportunities within GPC to export hydrogen in the future.

Speaking to The Observer of a trip to the company's biggest international customers in Japan, India and China in December 2017, Mr O'Sullivan said there were discussions on coal, hydrogen and growth in renewable energy.

"In 20 years' time Gladstone might be exporting hydrogen to Japan," Mr O'Sullivan said.

"We discussed being a partner with Japan, and other countries, it's very early days but from our perspective it's good to find out their interest in hydrogen as a future fuel," he said.

In the 2017-18 financial year, Mr O'Sullivan pocketed $533,000 in salary and $498,000 the year before.

Prior to his appointment, he had 14 years of experience with Gladstone Ports Corporation in community relations, human resources and major projects.

In 2009 Mr O'Sullivan was Labor's candidate for Gladstone in the Queensland Election.

He was unsuccessful in his attempt to unseat independent MP Liz Cunningham.

Mr O'Sullivan also worked as a project leader for the Western Basin Dredge and Disposal Project between 2010-2011, before working with PRM Consulting as a project director.

EARLIER: THE BOARD of Gladstone Ports Corporation have dismissed chief executive officer Peter O'Sullivan.

A media statement issued by the Corporation said Mr O'Sullivan had been under investigation since last year due to concerns raised about conduct.

Mr O'Sullivan was suspended on full pay since December 13.

GPC have announced Craig Walker will continue to serve as CEO in an acting position.

The timing of this decision comes a week after *The Courier-Mail* revealed the suspension of a GPC contractor working at the port, after asking former opposition leader Bill Shorten about tax cuts during the federal election campaign.

However, that week, the CEO spoke to the media, stating that while 12 allegations had been raised against him, only two were founded, and that his family had suffered as a result of the stress this situation had created. During his television interview, my husband was yelling at the television screen things like:

- 'You could've done the right thing.'
- 'We met with you twice to give you the opportunity to do the right thing.'
- 'You were in charge of your own destiny, and you didn't do the right thing.'
- 'You think your family has suffered – you should see what your choices have done to mine.'

This was the first time I could really tell how much those months of escalating, fighting, interviews and waiting had affected him. He had been stoic and silent alongside me and now was venting at the man that could have changed it all for the better.

The terminated CEO also posted a long rant on Facebook that identified people with either their names or initials, including matters and individuals who were the subject of investigation, which was a clear breach of confidentiality. I was very concerned that he was not accepting responsibility for his part in the process, and instead had turned to lashing out without consideration of the effect his actions would have with his apparent agenda to inflict the maximum damage to the remaining members of the Executive team. I was very stressed by his reckless behaviour as I was concerned it would negatively impact upon my family and I. Up until this point, I had very little respect for the terminated CEO and now I had none.

I still went into work the next day because I had a meeting planned with my new general manager to discuss my future career at the Corporation.

Batten Down the Hatches

I arrived at his office five minutes early to be advised by his executive assistant that he was too busy to see me. That was my breaking point. I think after going through the stress of the girl's treatment, the attempted cover-up, me escalating and being intimated by bogus serious claims being raised against me, being offered hush money, and then returning to work to be ostracised and now paid to do nothing without any future job prospects I just lost it. I walked out in tears, with shortness of breath, feeling like I needed to vomit and not in control of my body's functions. I now know this to be a panic attack.

> 'And once the storm is over you won't remember how you made it through, how you managed to survive. You won't even be sure, in fact, whether the storm is really over. But one thing is certain. When you come out of the storm you won't be the same person that walked in. That's what the storm is all about.'
> **Haruki Murakami**

CHAPTER 8

The Storm Front Builds

'You can't calm the storm so stop trying. What you can do is calm yourself. The storm will pass.'
Timber Hawkeye

I phoned my doctor's surgery, where I had been a patient for over 40 years, in tears and immediately made an appointment. I sat in the doctor's chair and offloaded everything to them. Instead of recounting the matters of the months leading up to this point, I recounted how it made me feel. Up until this point, I had been so driven and focused on the issues that I had not focused on my own emotions.

My doctor, a gentle soul who I normally visit with a sick child in tow, was my lifeline. He told me that based on the way I was feeling and the list of symptoms that I communicated that he thought I was suffering from anxiety and depression and that I needed medication. I was shocked because you hear about mental illness in the media all the time. I have friends and family that manage it on a regular basis, and I have been supportive of them over the years, but I had never experienced it myself and had no idea that the symptoms that were taking over my body without any notice were very serious. I had just called it stress until this point.

My doctor talked to me about the need for quality sleep and to calm my body's fight or flight mechanism – he noticed I had lost weight and appeared tired. He recommended that I take time off work and gave me a prescription to treat my symptoms. I took the Work Cover Medical Certificate and lodged the claim, but I asked if I could delay taking the medications a couple of weeks and instead receive mental health treatment. I told my doctor I was hoping that if I took time away from the workplace and started treatment that I could improve, because I did not want to take any antidepressant or other medication that may affect my brain's chemical balance. He agreed and asked me to contact him if I did not get into a psychologist straight away and to set a follow-up appointment.

****

I arrived at the office of the psychologist, called Superman, and when he invited me into sit in his consultation room, he handed me a questionnaire to complete so as he could understand how I was feeling. I do not remember the exact questions anymore; but as I filled out the list I was in tears. I was becoming emotional during the answers because it was listing how I had been feeling, and it was the first time I had stopped to think about it. I had been so focused on doing the right thing by myself, and by the young females, that I had not stopped to take care of myself.

Instead of me providing you misinformed, disjointed lists as I may recall them, please note the following list of the:

The Storm Front Builds

Signs and symptoms of anxiety:

- racing heart or tightening of the chest
- rapid breathing
- feeling tense, restless, 'on edge' or wound up
- hot and cold flushes
- sweating
- shaking
- feeling weak or tired
- obsessive thinking excessive fear and worrying
- having a sense of impending panic, doom or danger
- imagining the worst-case scenario
- having difficulty thinking about anything other than what's worrying you
- having trouble sleeping
- stomach or digestion issues
- avoiding situations that make you feel anxious (e.g. taking public transport, going to class or meeting new people)

Signs and symptoms of depression:

What you see:

- angry outbursts
- weight gain/loss
- withdrawing from close friends and family
- not participating in hobbies/activities
- skipping work, school or social activities
- not taking care of appearance and hygiene
- reckless behaviour
- not getting things done at work/school

Corporate Storm

What you don't see:

- difficulty sleeping or over-sleeping
- change in appetite, including comfort eating
- fatigue
- less interest in sex, intimacy issues
- low motivation, difficulty getting going
- muscle aches
- not enjoying activities you used to
- thoughts of self-harm or suicide
- negative self-talk
- headaches
- feeling down or 'numb'
- upset stomach
- feeling worthless, hopeless, angry or irritable
- difficulty concentrating or remembering things

Reference: www.reachoutaustralia.com

The first couple of sessions I had with Superman involved talking through the sequence of events and what had happened. As I recounted the facts this time, the difference was that he was most interested in how it made me feel. I sat in his consulting room each week able to speak for the first time about what had happened and how it had made me feel. He made me stop thinking for the first time, to accept where I was and to start to come to terms with how I was feeling. I had a psychology Superman on my support team now. I worked hard on every challenge he set and every reflection activity he tasked me with. Throughout this time, I was also called as a witness to the Treasury investigation for questions relating to the terminated CEO. In this interview, I obviously had a lot of information to provide. Then, a couple of months later, I was

The Storm Front Builds

interviewed in relation to the then-acting CEO. This development made me understand that the corrupt rot in the Corporation may run very deep and that I may never be able to return to work there. How do you work for someone you have been called to be a witness for, to provide information relating to their personal gain in their business dealings? Every time I was interviewed, I understood that the subject would be advised of my statements, so I only ever responded with information that I had evidence of.

To this day, I still do not understand how this acting CEO remained in the position whilst being the subject of a Treasury investigation. The terminated CEO was stood aside when he was a subject of the CCC investigation. I struggled with the disparity in treatment, but resigned myself to the fact that the Board and the State Government must have had their reasons for this decision.

At the same time as I was being interviewed by the Treasury investigation, the Corporation were continuing to make my life difficult by rejecting my Work Cover claim with excuses like:

- They had no control over the CCC or Treasury investigations.
- I was stressed out volunteering to run Australia's biggest fishing competition the past five years.
- I had been stressed out when my son fell from his bicycle and broke his C2 vertebra.
- The worst excuse where I knew they were really clutching at straws was when they said I had experienced great stress with my eldest daughter's cancer treatment, which she had undergone eight years prior.

During every step of this process, I tried to stay positive and focus on what was the personal growth I took from that experience, that interview, that psychology appointment and in this instance the Corporation's rejection of my claim. The acting CEO and HR GM were subjects of the investigations and were now a part of the problem. They were getting the opportunity to create further discomfort towards me. The act of them digging out a non-work-related matter from before my employment with them concerning my daughter undergoing cancer treatment many years prior as a part of their justification to reject my Work Cover claim highlighted to me that I had the resilience to continue to take on this fight against the big Corporation. I was the one person they had never encountered before – I did not care about my job. I had almost lost two children in my past, and my family, and my personal values take priority over everything, including a job.

I thought about walking away, but I felt empowered because I now had a psychologist providing me with the tools to accept the position I was in and to stop thinking about the 'what if?'. I did not know what the future had in store for me. Was I so mentally drained and damaged by this experience that I would never be able to work in a position of influence again? I had to get past the emotion and dig deep to work out how to correct this corrupt imbalance. I had to get further out of my comfort zone to do so.

I contacted both the CCC and Treasury investigation representatives and explained my position. They expressed their shock as to how my health had deteriorated, both saying that I was such a forthright, resilient and well-organised person to interview that they were surprised by how this had negatively affected me. They explained to me that the investigation's confidentiality clause did not encompass legal or medical advice. As I now know, writing this story from start to finish has been a cathartic part of my mental healing process.

In my order of life's priorities, I had nothing to lose but instead more to gain by continuing to expose these cronies for their dirty tactics. The big Corporation was not going to scare me away.

The Storm Front Builds

Sometime later, the Treasury representative phoned and advised that their team had met to discuss my situation and explained to me that under the CCC whistleblower legislation I was protected from reprisal action; however, a Treasury investigation witness has no protection. So, they recommended I agree to them sending a letter to the Corporation's Board to advise them of the reprisal actions I had received from the Corporation and the need to investigate them and ensure my protection. They outlined that the HR GM could not be privy to any matters relating to myself, nor the acting CEO.

I released my four-page letter of findings from the CCC to the work cover regulator and was sent to an independent psychiatrist for a medical assessment. As a result of these new items of information to support my claim the Work Cover file was accepted and I continued my regular appointments with my psychologist, Superman, and was referred to a psychiatrist who helped me to understand that my body had been under stress for that long that it had caused a chemical imbalance in my brain. Through working with my psychiatrist, I also began to understand that the reason for this stress was that in the past during my children Harrison and Annaliese's treatment, I had been supported by skilled and experienced specialists whose sole driver was to successfully treat sick patients. I had coped in these situations as I trusted their good intent. However, what I had encountered at the Corporation showed continual failure from the very top level. This caused distrust and me to feel unsafe – as they did everything they could to try to make me go away.

> *'Life isn't about waiting for the storm to pass; it's about learning to dance in the rain.'*
> **Vivian Greene**

CHAPTER 9

Storm Clean-Up

*'Just remember...there was calm before the storm...
there will be calm after.'*
Author Unknown

I accept that I will never know the outcome of the Treasury investigation. Rather, I hold onto the fact that the CCC investigation caused the removal of a general manager plus a CEO and triggered sweeping improvements at the Corporation in organisational development, corporate governance and reporting processes for fraud and corruption.

With the benefit of hindsight, I can now identify the characteristics of a storm brewing and identify where the Corporation neglected to adequately prepare for it.

Below are the 10 organisational challenges that can help you identify a harmful workplace culture where a storm may be brewing within your own organisation.

Corporate Storm

Is your organisation heading towards the perfect storm?

TABLE 1: 10 ORGANISATIONAL CHALLENGES

	Organisational Challenges	The Harmful Workplace Example
1	Inadequate or unimplemented management systems	No documented processes by which staff are held accountable. Verbal requests from Executive to officers. An environment of constant change, uncertainty, ambiguity, complexity and volatility. The strategic documentation (visions, missions, workplace values) makes for lovely posters on walls, but the ideas they represent are not integrated and alive in the workplace day to day. Most often, the Code of Conduct and Workplace Values manuals are used as weapons against employees.
2	No integration or alignment	Staff operate in silos and do not collaborate effectively. Tension and mistrust radiate throughout the organisation. Many matters escalate to the highest level to be resolved, and due to the lack of management systems the organisation is continually finding new ways of doing its business.
3	No REAL leadership	The above issues result in frontline leaders not being valued or given authority. Frontline leaders end up in a position where they cannot contribute their skills and knowledge in meaningful ways because they cannot connect the dots between tactics to strategy, vision to results, problems to solutions and ideas to outcomes.

Storm Clean-Up

	Organisational Challenges	The Harmful Workplace Example
4	Micromanagement	The Executive are continually involved in the daily operation of the organisation. Without setting the standards they need to continually be involved to make decisions, it results in the different levels and departments not trusting each other. It is hard to navigate the politics as you do not know who to trust, no one is ever invited to work collectively.
5	Deals done at the highest level	Commitments are made by Executives at meetings and informal settings with parties, and employees are then instructed to process the requests.
6	Cronyism	The Executives look after each other, including sweeping things under the carpet, such as the sexual harassment of young female employees. The Executives are lowest level of education and experience for their elevated positions and resent any challenge to their authority.
7	No one challenges leadership	Employees lack empowerment to speak the truth, create innovation or initiate improvement – 'Don't rock the boat.'
8	Fear obligation guilt by the executive	Any employee that 'steps out of line' to challenge the Executive is offered a payout to leave the organisation, of which the terms are to sign the Deed of Confidentiality and waive their rights to take any action in future.
9	Emotional blackmail	If the employee does not accept the payout to leave, then the Executive manufactures 'serious allegations that will result in an investigation.' Employees leave because they are fearful and need job security.

	Organisational Challenges	The Harmful Workplace Example
10	Lack of timely, quality, official communication from leadership	Workplace gossip fills the void. The Executive sometimes relies on gossip to disperse information where they do not wish to provide a clear and concise direction. The Executive does not effectively communicate information, priorities, expectations or changes in the organisation in a timely manner, or at all. In addition, many matters may be considered 'confidential' and the Executive uses this as a barrier to provide essential information while protecting the leadership and employee's anonymity.

Throughout my 12 months of CCC and Treasury investigation interviews, I was regularly provided with feedback from the interviewers that they had never met anyone as succinctly coherent as me to interview, or anyone with so much supporting evidence of their claims. This prompted reflection, and I realised that due to me having spent over 20 years in other large, multinational, privately owned organisations that have mature, integrated management systems within which to work, I naturally have a high professional standard and consistent, organised manner. This self-actualisation inspired me to write this part of the book because I could identify my personal workplace behaviours and understand why I did not go along with the corrupt flow or take the hush money to leave in fear – instead, I stood against the storm.

What is the storm preparation you can do to survive in a harmful workplace culture?

You need to circumnavigate the political storm by communicating for accountability.

TABLE 2: FIVE WAYS TO BEHAVE YOUR WAY THROUGH THE STORM

You can do this by behaving in these five ways:

1. Record communications – Keep evidence. Be disciplined with your document management and record-keeping, such as keeping a workplace diary. When provided with verbal instructions, follow up in writing with a summary of what has been discussed.

2. Grow influential relationships – Identify key social influencers across the organisation and understand what matters to them most.

Take the time to talk, socialise, discuss ideas, lobby for their support and think about what needs to be communicated to whom. Do not leave people out of the loop.

Organise conversations with decision-makers and stakeholders. Do not avoid opposing viewpoints, but rather take them on board to build better solutions. Create alignment.

3. Raise the professional maturity – Call out any dysfunction and facilitate conflict resolution rather than ignoring it and hoping it will disappear.

Be an empathetic listener. Be the person who creates solutions when there are differences of opinions.

You can work on helping other people to listen to each other.

4. Connect functions – Seek ways to cross-fertilise ideas and functions. Grow collaborative opportunities among people, teams, work groups and departments by involving them in conversations and meetings.

5. Recommend the engagement of external services to improve the culture – How many of the 10 organisational challenges outlined above in TABLE 1 are currently an issue in your organisation or team?

Take the test and ask yourself these questions:

TABLE 3: SELF TEST

#	Question Rating on a scale of 1-10	GOOD WORKING ORDER 1	NEUTRAL/ DON'T KNOW 5	PAINFUL & NEEDS FIXING 10
1	How severe is the pain you feel as a result of the harmful workplace culture?			
2	How severe is the negative impact on the organisation of the harmful workplace culture?			
3	How urgently does it need fixing?			
4	Is the harmful workplace culture causing the business to have problems with employee morale?			

Storm Clean-Up

#	Question Rating on a scale of 1-10	GOOD WORKING ORDER 1	NEUTRAL/ DON'T KNOW 5	PAINFUL & NEEDS FIXING 10
5	Is the harmful workplace culture causing the business to have problems with inefficiency in areas such as duplication of effort, delays and rework?			
6	Is the harmful workplace culture causing the business to have problems in not realising potential opportunities?			
7	Is the harmful workplace culture causing the business to have problems in trusting the Executive?			
8	Is the harmful workplace culture causing the business to have problems in earning a profit?			
9	Is the harmful workplace culture causing the business to have problems in employee turnover?			

10	Do you have the authority to make a decision to do something about improving the harmful workplace culture?	YES	NO
11	Do you think the harmful workplace culture can be improved?	YES	NO
12	Who else needs to be on a conversation about improving the harmful workplace culture?	List here:	
13	Which of the 10 organisational challenges (refer to TABLE 1) needs to be improved first?	List here:	

If your organisation's Executive ignores the 10 challenges that create a harmful workplace culture and hopes they just go away, the organisation runs the risk of these challenges expanding to cause larger issues in the future, including CCC investigations, legal claims and court cases.

'When the winds of change blow, some people build walls and others build windmills.'
Rishika Jains

CHAPTER 10

Skies Are Clearing

'Trust that the storm you are facing is here to help you become all you're capable of being.'
Author Unknown

The purpose of writing this book is not only to highlight some of the organisational challenges and the actions you can undertake to protect yourself in a harmful workplace, but also to spotlight building the necessary resilience to do so. I have come to realise that one of my strongest character attributes is my integrity. It is what drove me to continue through the overwhelming process and to write this book.

Integrity is one of those buzzword values that appears in every organisation's mission statement and position description. So, what does it mean in the context of the workplace? And how do you foster it in everyday actions?

Integrity is one of the core values that employers look for in potential employees. It is also a core value to a successful business operation.

To act with integrity is to ensure that every decision made is based on strong ethical and moral principles. Trust, honour and honesty are key elements to the concept of integrity. In the workplace, employees that act with integrity will always tell the truth, are accurate and factual, are accountable and reliable, and treat co-workers, stakeholders and customers with respect. They do the right thing, even when no one is watching because integrity is alignment between their words, actions and beliefs.

The thinking was over, and my emotional understanding began.

The part that I did not understand until I started to talk about what I had undergone with a psychologist was the emotions tied up in the situation. The emotional journey has been my biggest personal development and one that I wish to share, so others understand the emotional phases of my fight and what they can expect if they face their own corporate storm.

TABLE 4: EMOTIONAL PHASES OF THE FIGHT

	Phase	Mental health	What is it?
1	FRIGHTENED	Anxiety symptoms start	Being deterred from taking action, a fight or flight reaction.
2	ANGRY		Frustrated emotion of feeling powerless and being treated unfairly. How dare they? It is not honest.
3	REVENGE		Who can I blame? I am suffering and have not done anything wrong? Who can I get in return?
4	BARGAINING		Trying in vain to find a way out. Want the pain to go away.
5	OVERWHELMED	Depression creeps in	Why me? I have lost my career. My reputation has been damaged. A feeling of dread and despair envelopes. Very isolated, even from family and friends.
6	SHOCK	Mental health treatment	Stop thinking and start feeling. Reprogram the fatigued brain and reset it with less alarming thoughts.

	Phase	Mental health	What is it?
7	OPTIONS	Cognitive behavioural therapy	Find perspective. Find positive thoughts. Reprogram your brain. Adapt. Seek realistic solutions for a new future.
8	ACCEPTANCE		The fight is over, you cannot change it. Increased self-awareness to thoughts, body sensations and emotions. Start to become more reliable and confident.
9	REPURPOSE/ UPCYCLE/ NEW JOURNEY	Put yourself first	Find the good. No longer mourn the old me. Move from a victim mindset to a survivor mindset. What is my new reality? Try new things and implement a self-care routine. Writing a journal or this book to bring the thinking (what, where, who) in alignment with the feeling (how) to let go and explore all possibilities for the new future.

'The Devil whispered in my ear, 'You're not strong enough to withstand the storm.' Today I whispered in the Devil's ear, 'I am the storm.''
Author Unknown

Epilogue

I was away from the Corporation for a total of almost two years. During that time, the Corporation remained with an acting CEO at the helm. They went through three acting CEOs, turned over three commercial general managers and changed out the Chairperson twice. The organisation was unstable, with more people stepping up into higher duties to act in Executive positions compared to any permanent, experienced, high-calibre Executive. All the executives that handled my matters are no longer with the organisation and have all left our city. However, I have remained in our city, and I walk around town proud that I acted with integrity to trigger change that negatively impacted a few to benefit many.

I still stay in touch with the two young female trainees. One of these young ladies is pursuing her career in the commercial sector, married and has started a family. She read the draft of this book and encouraged me to publish it to expose what places like the Corporation are really like, and to hopefully inspire other people to gain the courage to do the right thing and change the path they are on. The other trainee has gone on to pursue her career in the mining sector and ironically is using the Rsured digital compliance management product in her workplace to handle all her training and risk management on the job. When she read this book draft, she was adamant it needed to be made available to the public. Over the years, she's been brave enough to talk to some people about her disgusting treatment while at the toxic corporation, and so she wanted this book published to empower others who have been silenced to speak out.

After standing up for what was right, I no longer had a desire to prove a point and return to an unstable workplace to become a part of the cultural change that I desired. So, just as I started the process myself, I ended the process myself, by resigning from the Corporation on my terms, with my final day being Australia Day. While I have captured many negative people and matters in this short story, I would like to acknowledge that these are a minority of the employees at the Corporation. There are many more good people working at the Corporation that I miss working with.

My husband has continued to work at the Corporation and hold his head high because he is proud of what we achieved. He has weathered the storm of gossip, rumours and innuendo that came along with the prolonged fight, and he has started to notice the many improvements that are being made within the business as they continue to try to find practical solutions in the development and integration of their business management systems.

The Corporation is no different to many other workplaces – namely, once a management system is implemented it uncovers non-compliance to be corrected and improved. My story highlights the opposition business face if they don't change-manage a management system implementation and have the direction and compliance of the executive to lead the way forward for the organisation.

Once I resigned, I handed all my information over to an employment lawyer so I could sleep at night knowing that nothing was ever lost, and I would regain my lost earnings and superannuation that I had sustained during the fight.

Epilogue

I now identify opportunities to go where I am celebrated, not just tolerated. So, I have continued volunteering in my community in not-for-profit organisations. In addition, I've joined Zonta International, a supportive community of likeminded professionals that stand for women's rights. I'm proud to have joined their Advocacy Committee to contribute to a more equitable world by empowering other women.

I've started my own management consulting business and am working with numerous clients both in the community and business sectors, one of which is Rsured for business compliance management. I've completed my Director Certificate and taken up Board positions to help community and private sector organisations with governance and compliance.

On a more personal note, over the years people have said to me that my family has been so unlucky. With our 13-year-old daughter fighting cancer and our 13-year-old son falling from his bicycle and breaking his C2 neck vertebrae. But I feel the opposite. My family are lucky because these challenges in life have brought us closer together and we value every day we experience life's ups and downs.

It is because of these challenges that my husband and I have built enough personal resilience and a strong partnership to not run away in fear, and instead face whatever life throws us front on and just put one foot in front of the other to keep moving forward together. So, when the Corporation turned a blind eye to the inappropriate treatment of two young girls, and offered to pay me hush money to leave, we knew there was only one path to take to be able to sleep at night: the path to fight for a just outcome and hold the corrupt executives responsible for their actions.

Our children are all proud of our efforts and are living healthy, active lifestyles. The experiences outlined in this book have helped our family grow stronger together.

Corporate Storm

Our family know the old sayings our grandparents used to tell us are all true:

1. Life is all about choices.
2. Anything good in life takes hard work.
3. If you tell the truth, you have nothing to hide.
4. Your family's health and wellbeing are your number one priority.
5. Don't let the fear of what could happen make nothing happen.
6. You only live once, so don't care about what other people think about you. Live your life the way you want to.

A final note: women's representation in senior leadership roles and on Boards has improved; however, there is still a long way to go to reach gender parity. At the same time, women at all levels of work still face numerous challenges, including unequal pay, intimidation, and harassment. As I finalise this book to send to the publisher, the insidious, entrenched corruption, bullying and harassment in the State and Federal Governments continue to make news headlines, and female politicians and employees continue to find their voice to speak out about their disgusting treatment.

Political commentators continue to demand that the leaders of our state and nation should be setting the standard high for the rest of us to strive towards.

The change starts with every one of us too. I can say I am an advocate to transform the workplace for women, and in writing this book I set a challenge for others to find their inner power to speak out. The more people that talk about this topic the less chance of the male cronies skirting around the truth, hiding the facts, and continuing. And, I have to say it, the less chance of the power-hungry or fearful females in leadership positions helping them to do so. Don't turn a blind eye and stay silent.

Finally, as my 94-year-old grandmother used to say, 'Don't be a part of the problem; be a part of the solution.'

Epilogue

Newspapers then started to cover the instability of the Corporation's governance and Executive turnover.

Thursday, Sep 30, 2021

By Anthony Marx

Dr Anthony Lynham quit politics a year ago but he's back to head the Gladstone Ports Corporation

Dr Anthony Lynham left state politics a year ago to focus on his medical practice but he starts a new job Friday as chairman of the troubled Gladstone Ports Corporation

A year after quitting state politics, Dr Anthony Lynham will return to the public sector Friday as the new chairman of the Gladstone Ports Corporation.

He'll be overseeing a troubled organisation buffeted by a recent series of internal management shake-ups, locked in several legal battles and subject to a possible corruption probe.

Dr Lynham, a former Natural Resources and Mines Minister, shocked colleagues after revealing in September 2020 that he would not recontest his seat of Stafford at the state election the following month.

After six years in parliament, he said that he could no longer juggle both a political career and a medical practice specialising in maxillofacial surgery.

"It has become very clear to me that I cannot maintain my medical registration as a doctor and give 100 per cent to this job," he said at the time.

Dr Lynham did not return calls seeking comment this week so it's unclear what has changed or how the new job will impact on his practice.

He'll be replacing Peter Corones, who has served as GPC chairman since 2018 and been on the board almost continuously since 1994.

His arrival comes just a month after the Crime and Corruption Commission revealed that it would embark on a two-year blitz focusing on councils, police and government departments in a bid to uncover wrongdoing.

The GPC was singled out as one of the potential targets of the inquiry, which will examine risks tied to nepotism in the recruitment process. It was formally put on notice that it may be audited.

The setback comes as the government-owned corporation continues to operate with a second transitional leader this year as the search continues for a permanent figure.

Current acting CEO Paul Heagney took over in August from interim chief executive Colin Cassidy, who spent just three months in the job.

The LNP raised questions in March about the role of Transport Minister Mark Bailey and his staff in the hiring process. The matter was referred to the CCC, which later cleared Bailey and his colleagues.

This drama came on the heels of the 2019 sacking of then-CEO Peter O'Sullivan and the resignation of three general managers the previous year.

Epilogue

O'Sullivan, who was ousted from the $546,000 a year job by the board over his handling of a staff disciplinary issue, denied he had acted improperly.

Meanwhile, the GPC is defending itself in a class-action lawsuit launched by more than 150 parties, mainly commercial fishermen and related entities chasing about $150m in damages.

They allege that their businesses were harmed after harbour dredging and other activities in 2011 polluted area waters and undermined the quality and quantity of fish.

An 11-week trial is expected to kick off in July next year.

The GPC is also fighting a lawsuit lodged in June by a former worker, who is seeking nearly $870,000 for a back injury he claims he got on the job.

The GPC, which also controls ports in Bundaberg and Rockhampton, has about 800 employees and generated more than $500m in revenue last year.

It reported an $81m net profit in the 2020 financial year.

Faced with the spectre of a CCC audit, Corones, Heagney, Cassidy and O'Sullivan have denied any wrongdoing.

CORPORATE STORM

THE OBSERVER

Wednesday, Dec 15, 2021

By Jacobbe McBride

The Australian Securities & Investments Commission launched their investigation into Gladstone Ports Corporation last week

The Australian Securities & Investments Commission launched their investigation into Gladstone Ports Corporation last week

The Gladstone Ports Corporation has acknowledged its referral to Australia's corporate watchdog over suspicions it has broken the law.

GPC was reported to The Australian Securities & Investments Commission by the Queensland Audit Office (QAO) late last week over potential noncompliance with legislation.

A QAO report tabled on December 10 found that GPC had spent $1,530,201 on six termination payouts since 2018, along with more than $10 million on legal costs in the 2020-21 financial year, almost double the cost of the previous financial year.

It also found that seven key management personnel and executives had left GPC since December 2018 and concerns were raised relating to the propriety of decision-making by the board and senior executives, including non-compliance with legislation, which would increase the risk of waste of public resources.

"In recent years, Gladstone Ports has had frequent changes to key management personnel and executive positions. These changes have negatively impacted on the governance structure, on reporting, and on the board's ability to enforce the desired decision-making culture," a summary of the report read.

"The changes to executives have also had a high financial impact, including six termination payments totalling $1,530,201 and related legal fees in 2020–21.

"The lack of policy, guidelines, and board oversight for these termination payments has raised concerns about the propriety of decision making."

The Audit Opinion results in the report also revealed Gladstone Ports was the only transport entity audited that did not meet its legislative deadline of August 31, 2021.

"The Gladstone Ports certification was delayed by management due to our request for additional assessments of the remuneration disclosures detailing salary and other benefits to ex-key management personnel," the report read.

"The financial statements were subsequently updated with additional disclosures relating to termination payments and certified on 14 September 2021."

A GPC spokesman said the business, which is a Queensland government-owned corporation, acknowledged the report by the QAO.

"GPC has committed to addressing recommendations, ensuring it remains an exceptionally performing state government owned port," the spokesman said.

"GPC remains committed to delivering for Queensland, with demonstrated performance and financial achievements in 2020/21, delivering more than $110 million to the State, including $20.6 million for initiatives backing maritime jobs in Queensland.

"GPC has a strong track record of running safe and busy ports to ensure we deliver sustainable economic growth and prosperity for the regions where we operate.

"GPC remains focused on governance and oversight, allowing the organisation to deliver on the priorities of jobs, trade and regional prosperity.

"The outlook for 2022 is very promising, with strong trade forecasts and demand for energy, particularly LNG."

The spokesman said GPC ports were featuring in considerations for developments in renewable energy, with emphasis on Green Ammonia and Hydrogen industries and export opportunities.

Queensland auditor-general Brendan Worrall said during the audit two matters raised concerns about the corporation's compliance under the Government Owned Corporations Act and the Commonwealth's Corporations Act.

He said in the report GPC did not initially provide a report to QAO or ministers about a payment to a former CEO.

Mr Worrall also said GPC failed to "appropriately approve and sign all board minutes".

"These compliance matters resulted in us reporting three significant deficiencies to Gladstone Ports," he said.

"We also reported the matters to the ministers and the Australian Securities and Investments Commission."

Mr Worrall made several recommendations to address shortcomings in Gladstone Ports' governance and oversight.

These included that policies be updated to provide guidance of payments through deeds of settlement and release.

Resources

PINPOINT	REFERENCE
1 Page 10	Port ripped off through their own scheme. (2017, April 3). *Gladstone Observer*. Retrieved from https://www.gladstoneobserver.com.au/news/breaking-port-ripped-off-through-their-own-scheme/3162567/
2 Page 12	GPC worker guilty on dodgy bbq claims. (2017, April 10). *Gladstone Observer*. Retrieved from https://www.gladstoneobserver.com.au/news/breaking-gpc-manager-let-off-lighter-than-workmate/3165230/
3 Page 14	BREAKING: GPC worker guilty on dodgy bbq claims. (2017, May 25). *Gladstone Observer*. https://www.gladstoneobserver.com.au/news/gpc-worker-busted-over-false-reimbursement-claims/3181598/
4 Page 16	Gladstone ports workers face court over false claims. (2017, July 12). *Gladstone Observer*. Retrieved from https://www.gladstoneobserver.com.au/news/workers-fined-for-false-claims/3199601/
5 Page 18	More GPC workers guilty of rorting health scheme. (2018, May 5). *Gladstone Observer*. Retrieved from https://www.gladstoneobserver.com.au/news/breaking-port-ripped-off-through-their-own-scheme/3162567/

6 Page 20	Business owner in GPC compensation rort faces $10,000 fine. (2018, November 17). *Gladstone Observer*. Retrieved from https://www.gladstoneobserver.com.au/news/business-owner-in-gpc-compensation-rort-faces-1000/3577887/
7 Page 23	Lawyer blames GPC "mismanagement" in compensation rort. (2018, December 3). *Gladstone Observer*. Retrieved from https://www.gladstoneobserver.com.au/news/lawyer-blames-gpc-mismanagement-in-compensation-ro/3591610/
8 Page 74	GPC remains tight-lipped on Zussino's role. (2017, August 18). *Gladstone Observer*. Retrieved from https://www.gladstoneobserver.com.au/news/state-govt-refers-gpc-matter-to-ccc/3496814/
9 Page 93	"It's normally an injury that you die of in a car crash". (2018, September 18). *Gladstone Observer*. Retrieved from https://www.gladstoneobserver.com.au/news/boy-breaks-neck-in-horror-bicycle-accident/3523633/
10 Page 96	"Special moment": Dog aids boy's recovery after crash. (2018, September 18). *Gladstone Observer*. Retrieved from https://www.gladstoneobserver.com.au/news/therapy-dog-aids-harrisons-recovery/3523639/
11 Page 98	Fuel mix up helps mum cope with son's near-death injury. (2018, September 18). *Gladstone Observer*. Retrieved from https://www.gladstoneobserver.com.au/news/fuel-mix-up-halts-mercy-dash/3523643/
12 Page 100	"Tears of joy": Mum recounts son's first steps after crash. (2018, 19 September). *Gladstone Observer*. Retrieved from https://www.gladstoneobserver.com.au/news/harrisons-long-road-to-recovery/3524595/

Resources

13 Page 102	Gladstone gets behind Harrison's recovery. (2018, 19 September). *Gladstone Observer*. Retrieved from https://www.gladstoneobserver.com.au/news/gladstone-gets-behind-harrisons-recovery/3524599/
14 Page 104	Crash victim Harrison is keen to get back home to Gladstone. (2018, September 21). *Gladstone Observer*. Retrieved from https://www.gladstoneobserver.com.au/news/harrisons-keen-to-get-back-home-to-gladstone/3526776/
15 Page 117	What's next for complaint about GPC. (2018, October 5). *Gladstone Observer*. Retrieved from https://www.gladstoneobserver.com.au/news/complaint-referred-to-treasury/3541405/
16 Page 121	Crime watchdog clears former Gladstone Ports Corp chairman. (2020, September 1). *Gladstone Observer*. Retrieved from https://www.gladstoneobserver.com.au/news/crime-watchdog-clears-former-gladstone-ports-corp-/4090495/
17 Page 124	Watchdog says Ports Corp inquiry "appropriate". (2020, September 1). *Gladstone Observer*. Retrieved from https://www.gladstoneobserver.com.au/news/watchdog-says-alleged-ports-corruption-inquiry-app/4090699/
18 Page 126	What Ports Corp said about CCC inquiry. (2020, September 2). *Gladstone Observer*. Retrieved from https://www.gladstoneobserver.com.au/news/what-ports-corp-said-about-ccc-inquiry/4091460/
19 Page 128	Ports boss sacked after complaint. (2019, May 21). *Gladstone Observer*. Retrieved from https://www.gladstoneobserver.com.au/news/gladstone-ports-ceo-peter-osullivan-sacked-after-c/3732733/

20 Page 130	"Grave concerns": Former ports CEO speaks out over sacking. (2019, May 21). *Gladstone Observer*. Retrieved from https://www.gladstoneobserver.com.au/news/grave-concerns-former-ports-ceo-speaks-out-over-sa/3733581/
21 Page 133	Ports Corp tight lipped on CEO saga. (2019, May 21). *Gladstone Observer*. https://www.couriermail.com.au/news/queensland/gladstone/business/gladstone-port-ceo-peter-osullivan-dismissed-by-board/news-story/48ba0215411a2a6dc0e026b097d28e16
22 Page 163	Dr Anthony Lynham quit politics a year ago but he's back to head the Gladstone Ports Corporation (2021, September 30). Courier Mail https://www.couriermail.com.au/business/qld-business/dr-anthony-lynham-quit-politics-a-year-ago-but-hes-back-to-head-the-gladstone-ports-corporation/news-story/946e5162465e0f7671e2db2b087b72b7
23 Page 166	The Australian Security and Investments Commission launched their investigation into Gladstone Ports Corporation last week. (2021, December 15). *Gladstone Observer*. https://www.couriermail.com.au/news/queensland/gladstone/the-australian-securities-investments-commission-launched-their-investigation-into-gladstone-ports-corporation-last-week/news-story/bb26a7723f62cf81a301126ced8acd49

Referrals

https://www.zonta.org/ Why Zonta?

We believe in making the world a better place by empowering women.

We find joy in doing this within a supportive community of like-minded professionals from diverse countries and cultures.

OUR CAUSES - Zonta stands for women's rights. We advocate for equality, education and ending child marriage and gender-based violence.

OUR PROGRAMS – Zonta expands opportunities for women and girls through our international education programs and service projects.

www.rsured.com Your Single Integrated Business Compliance Management System

SIMPLIFY COMPLEXITY – REDUCE RISK – IMPROVE PRODUCTIVITY – LOWER COST MANAGE COMPLIANCE WIN CUSTOMERS

rsured™ is an innovative, modular cloud platform that enables you to be in control anywhere, any time.

rsured™ integrates and automates your business management systems and provides customisable dashboards to reduce complexity and improve efficiency.

www.ag.gov.au/rights-and-protections/human-rights-and-anti-discrimination/respect-at-work ENOUGH IS ENOUGH

A Roadmap for Respect: Government Response to Respect @ Work Report

On 8 April 2021, the Australian Government released 'A Roadmap for Respect: Preventing and Addressing Sexual Harassment in Australian Workplaces' (Roadmap for Respect).

The Roadmap for Respect responds to all 55 of the Australian Human Rights Commission's recommendations outlined in the Respect@Work report. The Roadmap for Respect provides a clear and comprehensive path forward for Australia to prevent and address sexual harassment and support meaningful cultural change in our workplaces.

The Government has formed **The Respect@Work Council** (the Council) brings together leaders from key government regulators and policy-makers responsible for sexual harassment to improve coordination, consistency and clarity across existing legal and regulatory frameworks, and to identify ways to promote safer workplaces.

The Council held its first meeting on Friday 19 March 2021.

www.beyondblue.org.au Beyond Blue

Provides support on a range of mental health issues and is available by phone 1300224636, online via chat or email.

www.1800respect.org.au 1800RESPECT

Healthy relationships start with feeling respected and safe.

You have a right to respect and safety in all your relationships.

Relationship behaviour that is abusive is never OK and it may be domestic and family violence or sexual violence.

If you are worried about unhealthy, abusive or violent behaviour in any of your relationships, you can contact 1800RESPECT on 1800 737 732

Jennifer McGuire

is the whistleblower who cracked open a corrupt Government Owned Corporation Executive. It became her mission to represent young females that had been sexually harassed and bullied. She didn't turn a blind eye to take the hush money secret deal and sign a non-disclosure agreement to silence her. Instead, she took the fight to them. In the process, she discovered so much more...

An engaging and motivating speaker, Jennifer will reveal her shocking personal battle and provide you with firsthand insight to understand if your organisation is heading towards a Corporate Storm, what you can do about it and, most importantly, how you can survive it.

Jennifer delivers serious organisation-changing messages in a personable, accessible way by easily connecting with any audience with her warm and conversational style.

She finally shares her story after sitting quietly, waiting to be heard because of the Crime & Corruption Commission and Treasury investigations that ensued. She discloses about what she did and demystifies the serious, elevated investigation processes.

With over 25 years of extensive professional experience in leadership positions, built on a solid foundation of business academic knowledge, Jennifer understands that relevant stories and practical examples are crucial to the success of your event, with a key take-home message to promote further learning and growth.

Tailoring her talk to the interests of your organization and your audience, Jennifer works with both intimate groups and large auditoriums.

She can communicate for change with all levels of an organization by tailoring to:

1. Employees and team members
2. Managers and frontline leaders
3. Executive and the Board

Engage Jennifer for a presentation, team-building workshop, awareness-raising talk, or a more interactive seminar that is guaranteed to be interesting, engaging and a catalyst for change.

Please contact: Jennifer McGuire
✉ info@corporatestorm.com.au
🔗 www.corporatestorm.com.au

About the Author

Jennifer McGuire is a happily married mother of two daughters and two sons. Since graduating university with a Bachelor of International Business majoring in Economics, she has worked in leadership roles in major corporations for over 25 years. While on parental leave after the birth of each of her children, she undertook further study through Advanced Diplomas in Project Management, Export Management and Frontline Management to ensure she stayed at the top of her game and progressed her career. She and her husband have made an effective team, with him thriving as a stay-at-home dad for five of those years.

Jennifer has always believed in investing in youth and has been inspired to lead with her coaching and mentoring skills to provide school leavers a traineeship to lead to future job opportunities. She finds it deeply rewarding when previous trainees reach out to seek career advice or ask her to be a reference.

About the Author

Jennifer is a strong believer in on-the-job training and studying as a part of career development. She has been recognised with the Australian Institute of Management's Manager of the Year and Rio Tinto Global Leadership Talent awards.

Jennifer has a successful track record of challenging male executives to encourage diversity in the workplace. She has created and contributed to many equal employment opportunity initiatives over the decades. For example, during a presentation in which she was recommending a paid parental leave policy, she asked a production manager how he would feel if he fell pregnant. To imagine if he was the person who had been gifted with a uterus and had a baby. To think about how he would feel when he returned to work and his employer couldn't guarantee his previous position because of the lack of a parental leave policy which meant he had to take a step down in his career by returning in an assistant capacity. This struck a chord by making the entire male management team consider how the absence of such a policy affected their female employees, and so the policy was approved.

When she first started in Big Industry almost 30 years ago, Jennifer wore men's gloves, trousers, shirts and boots that were all unfit for purpose as they were so large that they enveloped her feminine body. Over the years, Jennifer has championed income parity between male and female employees performing the same job, set up female amenities to encourage mothers to return to work, and mentored many young women starting out their careers.

In authoring this book, Jennifer hopes it will encourage young women to require, particularly male executives to provide a safe and respectful place to work. She has had *ENOUGH!*

Jennifer believes that many of society's issues would be resolved if more men were involved in raising children to the degree women are, allowing women to be equal actors outside the home.

www.ingramcontent.com/pod-product-compliance
Lightning Source LLC
Chambersburg PA
CBHW021148080526
44588CB00008B/255